THE LUNCH-BOX CHRONICLES

Also by Marion Winik

Telling

First Comes Love

THE
LUNCH-BOX
CHRONICLES

Notes from the

Parenting Underground

MARION WINIK

PANTHEON BOOKS   NEW YORK

All rights reserved under International and Pan-American
Copyright Conventions. Published in the United States by
Pantheon Books, a division of Random House, Inc., New York,
and simultaneously in Canada by Random House of Canada
Limited, Toronto.

Portions of this work were originally published in *Harper's Bazaar,*
Parenting, and *Redbook.*

Library of Congress Cataloging-in-Publication Data

Winik, Marion.
The lunch-box chronicles : notes from the parenting
underground / Marion Winik.
p.   cm.
ISBN 0-375-40156-3
1. Single-parent family. 2. Parenting. 3. Single parents.
4. Winik, Marion. I. Title.
HQ759.915.W58 1998
306.85'6—dc21
97-26753
CIP

Random House Web Address: http://www.randomhouse.com

Book design by Mercedes Everett

Printed in the United States of America

First Edition
2   4   6   8   9   7   5   3   1

For Nancy

THE LUNCH-BOX CHRONICLES

IN SCHOOL PORTRAITS tacked over my desk, you can see them at seven and five: Captain America and his little brother, the Refugee. Hayes makes a smirky Captain in his blue Cub Scout uniform and shiny helmet of hair, arms folded statesmanlike on the desk before him. Poor Vincent could qualify for social services on the basis of this photograph alone, I fear, eyelids half-mast, face covered with boo-boos, one ear blending with some books on a shelf in the background so that it looks outsized and deformed, like a leaf of radicchio.

How is it that these school mug shots can turn the most photogenic little angel into a sickly goon who seems to be smiling despite the matchsticks wedged under his fingernails? And the prices! I'll take the Bargain Bonanza Package for forty-five bucks, please. Couldn't pass up those two dozen bonus wallets.

"Dear Mom," says an old Mother's Day letter posted beside the photos, written in shaky, fresh-minted cursive handwriting on blue-lined paper. "I really like when you take me to the movies. You are

3

special because you cook what I like. I want to help you clean the house. I really like how you smile. I have a surprise for you. Love, Hayes."

He wanted to help me clean the house? That was surprise enough. Another missive is penciled on a bunny cut out from yellow construction paper: "Dear Mom. I love you Mom. Happy Spring Break Mom. When can Will come over."

Vincie, who doesn't write letters yet, is represented by artwork: a penciled depiction of a Martian and his pet shark, living in a castle full of fax machines and Nintendo controllers; another sheet printed all over with a rubber stamp of Vincent Winik's return address, some wobbly pink hearts, two figures with big smiles and bifurcated flippers for arms, and one word: MOM.

Some days—like maybe three out of a hundred— I am just so busy riding a tsunami of productivity in this home office of mine, I wish I didn't have to drop everything at 2:40 in the afternoon to go pick up my little pals at school. Far more likely, I start checking the clock at eleven, if not before, and count the minutes until it's time to go. Not only because it means I get to escape the solitude of the so-called creative process for a few hours and resume my role as household drudge, math tutor, and nuthouse warden, but because I can't wait to see them, to repossess them, to get them back on my territory, whole, healthy and breathing—in part, the same impulse that used to drive me to check their baby cribs midnap. Of course, this feeling of anticipation involves a bit of willful tiptoeing around the possibility of the Awful Afternoon with the Devil Brats from Hell, but hey, why not be optimistic.

I fly out the door and into the Jeep and have to force myself to slow down to twenty miles per hour as I reach the speed bumps and blinking lights of SCHOOL ZONE. I pull into the circular drive of the brick elementary school behind the minivans and Volvos and pickup trucks, and my personal favorite, the flower-power-printed Volkswagen Beetle that belongs to a local family doctor, reportedly equipped with a car phone but no air conditioning.

On the bench under a live oak tree, a mom with a Keith Haring button and black leggings is chatting amiably with a dad in a three-piece suit. Baby brothers and sisters mill around as their mothers stand in clusters, deconstructing last night's PTA meeting with the earnestness of Harvard graduate students, and representatives from various after-school programs stand ready with clipboards to gather up their broods. I spy the fund-raising coordinator and wander over to find out when I'm scheduled to sell grocery certificates but am waylaid en route by the soccer coach and the plant sale chairwoman. BRYKER WOODS ELEMENTARY, says my mental bumper sticker for this place. WHERE PARENT INVOLVEMENT IS A SICKNESS.

The hair-raisingly loud buzzer euphemistically known as the "bell" goes off, the blue-green doors fly open, and the kids start tumbling out: the kindergarteners with their toy-store backpacks and Velcroed sneakers, who already look so tiny to me; the unimaginably grown-up sixth graders, with skateboards and cellos and streaks of orange dyed into their hair; and all the many kids from grades between who wear the same haircut as my kids do, so that almost daily, at least for a fraction of a second, I mistake someone else for mine.

And I'm still searching the crowd when one of them skids up in front of me: my first grader Vince, his six-and-a-half-year-old body coltlike, skinny and knobby under the baggy, faded, torn-up, mismatched clothes he would rather die than throw away. Though he seems to get taller almost daily and can prepare a can of chicken noodle soup from start to finish without assistance, his face still wears the heart-tuggingly pure expression of one who has not completed the transition from baby to boy: something in his round blue eyes and jutting pink lower lip is as radiantly unformed, as clear and open, as it was when he was an infant waking up in his bassinet. He refuses to tie his shoes or get out of bed in the mornings, he has a wide lazy streak, a thirst for sibling combat, a madman's scream, and a whine that could probably serve as a form of torture in a pinch, but you can still see the otherworldly sweetness that he came with from the factory, which had his father and me insisting half-seriously to our acquaintances that we had given birth to the Baby Messiah.

"Can Calvin come home with me?" the former baby messiah wants to know. "Please, Mom, please, he really wants to."

"Well, I'd really love him to, too, but you know we have to make plans with his mom the night before we want to have him over."

"I *never* get to have anyone over!" says Vince, resorting to his favorite negotiation strategy, what surely must be Chapter One in the six-year-olds' edition of *The Art of the Deal*. "You *always* say no! You *never* let me do anything!" He folds his arms and pushes his lower lip as far out as it will go, a key element of this diplomatic technique.

"Vincie, there's nothing I can do about it. If we don't make advance arrangements so his mom can send a note, she gets fined by the whatchamacallit place he's supposed to go."

"All right," he exhales grumpily, and turns to go report the bad news to Calvin. The first three steps are an exaggerated shuffle of despair, then he lapses back into the usual skip. When he returns, I am gazing at him with a goofy smile of adoration.

"How come you look so happy today?" he asks me suspiciously. He asks me this almost every day.

"You know why," I say.

"Because you're so happy to see me?"

"Yup," I say, "that's why." And then he looks at me with an expression that is half pleased, half embarrassed ("That Mom. She's a moron, but she's *our* moron") and gives me a quick hug. Just because I still can, I grab him, whoosh him up in the air and bounce him over to the car, and he's grinning from the sheer fun of being tossed around.

"Okay," I say, "where's your brother?" I visually pick through the jumble of kids turning somersaults on the bike rack, others tossing a football on the lawn.

"Mommy," says Vince—who is a chatterbox given to long, often confusing monologues, and something about this "Mommy" seems to herald one—"guess what happened? Frederick got sent to the North Pole because he wouldn't stop talking during story and all the other boys got in trouble too butcept me and Mrs. Harverstick came and gave me a sticker and—"

It kills me when he says "butcept." But I must interrupt.

"Vincie, go get Hayes," I order, spotting his

brother engaged in some important third-grade pow-wow with two friends. "See him back there by the fence?"

"But don't you want to see my sticker?"

"Of course I do, sweetie. Oh, wow! That's great! Now go get Hayes."

"Hayes!" Vincie bellows without moving an inch.

Hayes, whose ears have somehow picked up the brother frequency over the din of the schoolyard, says goodbye to his friends and comes toward us. He's wearing his blue-and-white Dallas Cowboys jersey, matching navy shorts and a pair of oversized white high-tops that are endorsed by, and indeed almost look as if they would fit, Hakeem Olajuwon. His hair still shows a trace of the spray gel I was begged to comb in this morning to make it stay over to the side like that of a currently idolized classmate. Unlike his little brother, Hayes at nine is all the way to boy, and sometimes beyond: his handsome, longish face already wears the ironic expression that his father's did, amusement playing around the mouth, but a seriousness, a certain concern, in the warm brown eyes.

"Hey, Mom," he says, his eyes on a cluster of friends roughhousing nearby. He reaches to tweak the backpack strap of a passing buddy.

"How was school today?"

"Great," says Hayes. That's what he always says.

That's what they all say. The public schools could be teaching guerrilla tactics, animal husbandry or Sanskrit grammar all day and the parents of America would be the last to know.

"Can you be more specific? Did anything interesting happen? If I'm not going to get a hug, could we at least make eye contact?"

He gives me a grin and a quick hug. Score! But wait, there's more: "Mom, can we stop and get a Slim Jim or something? I'm starving half to death!"

"Me, too," Vincie chimes in at his elbow, looking to see if Brother Boss Man has noted his helpful contribution to the hunger relief effort.

"Get in the car and put on your seat belts," I command.

"But Mom, it was Sloppy Joes for lunch and it was so gross I couldn't even eat it."

"All right, all right! We'll stop at the store! Now come on, let's get going. How much homework do you have? Hey! Stop playing with that ball in the car! I can't drive! Put it away! Do you want to go to the store? Then put the ball in the back seat! Now!"

No one is paying any attention to me at all. Well, I'm used to it. I reach one arm back, knock the ball away, start the car and ease out into traffic. The afternoon sun is in my eyes, but I can't find my sunglasses in the heap of army men, half-melted crayons and cassette boxes beside me. The boys are punching each other, Hayes is singing "Nacho Nacho Nacho Man, I want to be a Nacho Man" over and over in a monotone, Vincie's backpack is full of gravel and dirt which he's dumping out on the seat of the car, and we're on our way to the grocery store to get Slim Jims and a box of macaroni.

I'm with my boys, and all is right with the world.

1

Nuclear Disaster, with Macaroni

Once upon a time, I had a normal family. Well, maybe not a normal family—I doubt the Winiks, party of four, were ever mistaken for that mythical creature—but we were at least biologically classic: a man, a woman, and their two begotten children. Yes, phantasmagoric as it seems to me now, for the first six years of parenthood, I had a husband. A helpful husband, I might add, one innately, charmingly at ease with diapers, car seats, bottle brushes, wooden blocks, rubber ducks, and Clorox Two.

Though progressive in this and other aspects, our four-cornered family matched the geometry of the families I grew up with. Back in the sixties and seventies, we didn't know many divorced people. We didn't know many "blended" families either, probably because there weren't enough broken ones to match up and stick back together. The basic shape of the family was a square—mommy, daddy, and two kids—or perhaps a pentagon or an octagon if the family was Catholic. Almost as rare as a divorced parent in those days was a family with only one child. Widowed parents I never even heard of.

Somehow during those six years of yuppie innocence after my children's birth, I lived in a world with some similarity to the one I grew up in. Except for one woman, the primigravidas in the mothers' support group I joined after Hayes was born were living with the fathers of their new babies, and most were married to them. We were a covey of sweet newborn families, wholesome as the bread we baked and the cloth diapers we righteously used. Our one single mom (who was unbelievably also saddled with a permanent limp) I regarded as a saint. Any time I heard her stories, or read about single parents in magazines or the newspaper, I reacted with a mixture of admiration and horror. "It's unfathomable," I would say. "I could never do it."

In case I hadn't made myself clear to any forces of destiny who might be listening, I would repeat for emphasis: "Never!"

By 1992, when it began to be clear to just about everyone except me that my husband Tony's escalating battle with AIDS was bound to be lost, these pronouncements of mine tended to elicit a perturbed reaction. Surely I knew what was awaiting me. Surely I heard the irony. Surely I couldn't have been in that much denial.

Well, actually I was, thank you very much. And I liked my fluffy pink denial, too. Any extra untroubled weeks it won me I was happy to have, smiting my brow and calling the single mothers saints, rather than taking a closer look at how they were getting by and trying to picture myself among them. But eventually—I guess it was around the day Tony moved into the AIDS hospice—I had to face the facts.

My reaction was: Holy shit.

As spoiled as I was, no one could have been more terrified of single motherhood than I. After all, I had been raised in a family not only with two parents, but with a live-in maid. And while I had not replicated this setup in my adult life, there was really no reason to miss it. Tony did his share of the kidwork and housework, and more. Now was I going to have to do everything myself? Every meal, every pile of wet sheets, every Christmas tree, every sink, every sticky, littered, crumb-covered, upside-down disaster area? Every tuck in, wake up, drop off, round up, and drive home—for the next fifteen years?

My life stretched before me like a hard labor sentence. And if I didn't feel sorry enough for myself about that, it got worse: Not only would I be stuck with all the work and all the financial responsibility, but I'd have no one to talk to. I would have no partner, no companion, no lover, no buddy. By any emotional definition I knew, I would be alone.

I had never lived by myself. I had never wanted to live by myself. In fact, I had never really wanted to spend more than about ten minutes—one hot shower's worth—by myself. And now, though not alone in fact, I would be in a situation perhaps even more unpleasant. Not just without adult company, but enslaved, subjugated and constrained by the needs of two young and helpless housemates. Many of the little privileges of the solitary life—the sacrosanct bathroom, the odds-and-ends fridge, the late dinners of frozen yogurt eaten half naked in front of Letterman—would not be available to me. In fact, I would be living "alone" in an unusually excruciating form, with all of the loneliness and none of the self-indulgence.

I'd have no one to ramble to while I did the dishes and no one to cast a pleading look at when I wasn't up to them. No one to answer the phone if I was in the bathroom. No one to hold down the fort while I ran out to the movie store—in fact, I'd be lucky if I ever left the house after eight-thirty at night again. On the parenting front, too, I'd be on my own. No one to gloat with over report cards or fret with over bed-wetting, no one to share the news if the annual well-check turned up a problem.

Didn't anyone hear me when I said never?

Hayes and Vince, four and six at the time of their father's death, turn seven and nine this year. And fine young men they are, I'm happy to say. Most of the grace with which we've gotten through these past three years has come from them. They seem constitutionally unable to dwell on the past or to feel sorry for themselves for more than a minute or two, and their energy for the project of getting on with it, for growing up, has been a miraculous ace in the hole. Come *on*, Mom, they're always saying, both literally and metaphorically, so I just can't seem to find time to fall apart and be a victim, when there are soccer practices to go to, rocks to collect, friends to have over, Cub Scout banquets in desperate need of my baked ziti.

"If Daddy was alive, he would come on my class skating trip," Vince said matter-of-factly a few months ago. "But you'll come instead, right?"

Even though his father was a professional ice skater and I am a professional klutz, he was right about that.

"Good!" said Vince. His face clouded for a minute. "I wish Daddy could come."

I hugged him close. "I do too, baby. I do too."

After a second, he pulled away. "Can you help me find my hat with the blue ponpon?"

"Pompom, Vincie," I say.

"That's what I said! Ponpon!"

When I look at single mothers with infants—who really are saints, I still think—I must acknowledge that the duration of the "hard labor sentence" I so feared was very short. Hayes and Vince were out of diapers when we started this arrangement, and now already take out the garbage and walk to the corner for a jug of milk. Hayes can work the coffeepot—he made a chart with illustrations to help him remember the steps—and they both know exactly how Mommy prefers her morning cup. (Pitch black and flat on her back.)

There's a certain romance to the relationship between a single parent and his or her children. It's not just they who rely solely on me, but I who depend quite heavily on them as well. Without a separate adult world to retreat to, I spend more time cultivating their company. It's a major difference. Would I have been holed up in a Holiday Inn in New Iberia, Louisiana, watching *Forrest Gump* with the kids last March if I'd had a husband to plan spring vacation with? Would I invite them to sleep in my king-size bed on cold winter nights? Would I be conferring with Hayes to develop strategies for getting Vince out of bed in the morning, or thinking of fun things for me and Vince to do while Hayes is away for the weekend on a camping trip? I don't know what Freud would make of it (or the boys' future therapists, for that matter), but they are my sweethearts in a very real way.

See? Not so alone after all.

But just feeling closer to the kids is not enough to make this single-parent thing work, and too much closeness without a break would probably backfire. A person would be not just a saint but a martyr if she spent so much time taking care of other people without getting taken care of herself. Fortunately there is a long list of grown-ups who cook the dinners, buy the movie tickets, drive the car pools and give the foot massages that save me from the never-very-threatening prospect of canonization, who keep my perceived aloneness at a level I can bear. They take my kids places, take me places, include us all in their excursions—they fill the empty spaces in one-parent life. I would be lost without my friends and neighbors, without my mother and my in-laws, without all the parents from the various classes, teams and troops, without babysitters, without my boyfriend Robb, a divorced dad himself, with two daughters.

The divorced are single parents yoked together, and believe me, they don't want to hear my complaints. Even if I don't have someone to take my kids off my hands every other weekend or pay half their upkeep, I also have—they point out—no one to negotiate with, no one to argue with me about money, no one to steal my kids over Thanksgiving weekend or take up with a twenty-two-year-old bimbo who alienates their affections. No one whose ever-present pain-in-the-ass behavior destroys my happy memories of my perfect past. And if I want to go somewhere with the kids, I just get in the car and go. If I want to buy them something, I just go to the store and buy it. I'm free. I'm the boss. What I say goes.

Well, that's true, but on the other hand, my kids don't have a father anymore. I hate it that Tony never saw Hayes play soccer, or heard Vince read aloud. I dread going to teacher conferences alone. It breaks my heart every time I leave blank the line that says "Father" on application forms, and bedtime stories and movies with major daddy themes are never easy. While living daddies are bad enough, supposedly dead daddies who come back to life are about the worst, and there are a startling number of these out there, I am sorry to report. Furthermore, there is no way I can help my sons carve their wooden cars for the annual Pinewood Derby (which I keep wanting to call the Pinebox Derby, as if the Cub Scouts were rolling coffins down the street), though I doubt Tony would have been much help with that either.

But every year, there's someone who can, and does. Like free radicals in chemistry, we single-parent families tend to bond, and only-child families stick themselves on too, and people without children sometimes show up for a visit. We even let the picture-perfect clans with 2.5 in the Plymouth Voyager come along, though they seem to get rarer all the time. Of the mothers in my old support group, nine years down the road from the time when we were all but one happily partnered, five more of the original dozen are now on their own. I'm widowed, four are divorced, and two of the remaining married women have husbands who are seriously ill. The old photographs seem like pictures from another life.

Yet we stick together, we odd-lot households, relying on the superglue that is our love for our children to fit our families together in ways that don't necessarily match the picture on the box. What we want for them is what we want for ourselves as well: if not the image of a happy family, at least the spirit of one, the warmth and tolerance of people who care about each other. With the tough lessons of our disappointments and mistakes behind us, and the wide-eyed trust of the children we've taken with us from the wreckage, perhaps we splinters are as qualified as anyone to make it work after all.

If there is a secret of single parenthood, I think it's this: It's amazing what you can do when you have no choice. Amazing what you'll call dinner when there's no other adult watching. Amazing how many consecutive days a boy will wear the same pair of shorts, or how quickly he takes to a stint in the after-school program. Once you give up on perfection, on doing it "right"—and you might as well, since as a single parent you're substandard and wrong by definition—you find the whole thing goes a lot more smoothly.

For example. 5:30 P.M. Do you know where your children are? Sure, they're at the school or the day care center and you are in rush hour traffic, fighting your way across town to retrieve them. So unfortunately by the time you get home, there will be no time to prepare a delicious nutritious home-cooked meal like your mother supposedly used to make, and once again you've neglected to whip up an entire week's worth of casseroles on Sunday afternoon. Assaulted from all sides by the cries of starving youth, you will have time to do no more than open a can of soup, stuff some hot dogs in the microwave, dump the feel that faster and easier may actually be better. I have arrived at this conclusion the hard way. On those occasions when I have tried to be the kind of parent who melts her own cheese, who serves at least one item from each food group attractively arranged on a plate, my children almost always curl their lips, spill their milk, maroon their forks in the rice pilaf and offer some flattering comment such as: How many bites do I have to eat to get a popsicle? There were a few successes in there, I'll admit, but in some ways I only felt stupid about being so dad-gum thrilled to see my children eat a slice of meat loaf. Ultimately, I have accepted the following principle of subsistence-level parenting: *The more time you spend on something, the less your kids like it.*

Dinner is just one example of this phenomenon. If you have ever sewed a Halloween costume, baked a birthday cake from scratch, packed something fun and creative in your child's lunch box, or tried to get him to wear the sweater your mother knitted for him last Christmas, you know that kids hate homemade. They want prepackaged. They want standard issue. They want logos and brand names. Most importantly, they want to be like everyone else. And even when they see you weeping on the kitchen floor because their reaction to your fresh-from-the-oven fruit bars is "Uh . . . do we have any Oreos left?" they still don't cheeseburgers out of the bag, or dial the well-worn number of the closest pizza place.

Obviously this is an area where S, M, D, and W parents find common ground. As I tell myself when I load my cart with three-for-a-dollar boxes of instant macaroni and cheese, they wouldn't manufacture these things in bulk and stock shelf upon shelf of them at the supermarket if great hordes of people didn't buy them, if millions of parents out there didn't breathe a sigh of relief as they dump the quote-unquote cheese out of a paper packet rather than grate and melt the genuine article. Apparently I'm not the only person who thinks having the pasta premeasured and the instructions printed on the package instead of in a hard-to-reach cookbook with stuck-together pages makes the hairline difference in stress level that keeps one out of the local psychiatric hospital. Have you seen the salad that comes in the plastic bag with the lettuce already washed? The broccoli with the stems cut off? The premarinated chicken breasts? This is not just the food of convenience. It is the food of mental health.

While knowing that I am not the only one who doesn't have the time or energy to accomplish basic parenting tasks with any sort of style makes me feel a little better, deeper solace comes from the following. Call it a rationalization if you must, but I sometime get it. The perfect lunch, as far as they're concerned, is one that comes ready-made from the grocery store, thoroughly swathed in plastic and stamped with large red letters that say *Lunch. Just for Kids. Only $4.99.*

Let us focus for a minute on the birthday party, surely the most anxiety-ridden moment of the year for the underachieving parent. To do or to spend: this is the question. Surely it is nobler in the mind to cut paper garlands, bake and decorate cupcakes, fashion party favors with your own two hands. But with fast-food outlets, Celebration Stations, Chuck E. Cheeses and Discovery Zones angling for your birthday dollar, and your children begging piteously for you to give it to them, the temptation to take the easy way out is severe. Even if you have the time or inclination for a good old-fashioned birthday at home, your kid doesn't want it. They want a store-bought party: an afternoon at Peter Pan Putt-Putt, Laser Quest or Malibu Grand Prix. Quaint is out. Prefab is in. Sometimes you just have to go with the flow. You may have hearing loss and brain damage afterwards, but you will be able to say those four precious words: The kids loved it.

Of course these insta-birthdays aren't cheap. It costs money to be a lazy parent, and to make that money you're going to be a busy parent. Between lazy and busy, you cannot afford to devote another minute to guilt. So stop with the angst. Sit down and unwrap that cheeseburger with a smile. Deliver the store-bought muffins to the bake sale with your chin held high. Why not go one step further? Get your kids to start doing some things for themselves! For you, even. You will notice that shortly after you stop popping out of bed on Saturday morning to make breakfast, they learn to pour cereal without assistance. Once they get this much down, good news: mastering the operation of the coffee machine is not far behind.

Kids are realists. They know which parents in the neighborhood do fun art projects at home, which are good at soccer, which allow unlimited Nintendo and which come through with the homemade chocolate chip cookies. Me, I'm the Old Widow Winik with her box macaroni and her freeze pops, and let me tell you, I usually have quite a crowd for dinner.

Unfortunately not all the lessons I have learned in grocery stores were as pleasant as this. While I've made my peace with dinner-in-a-box, one of the most deeply unsettling moments in the past few years happened in the bakery aisle.

2

The Uses of Prayer

The trip to our neighborhood grocery store seemed completely ordinary at the outset. As usual, as soon as we stepped through the electric doors, Hayes and Vince, seven and five at the time, made a beeline for the bakery, where they availed themselves of the store's generous "one free cookie per kid" policy. Booty in hand, they repaired to the nearby café tables where they would hang out and look at comic books while I cruised the aisles—a recently established ritual which had made grocery shopping more enjoyable for all of us.

It took me a little longer than usual that day to figure out which brand of paper towels to buy, which size of egg, which flavors of frozen juice concentrate, and—deep breath—whether we would prefer kosher pickles, dill pickles, or kosher dills, a decision that can really cause brain damage if you don't watch it. Even as I wrestled with the usual options, out of the corner of my eye I noticed something "New!"—a variety labeled "crunchy kosher dills." Was "crunchy" anything like "Polish"? Or was it more like "garlic"? And what did this mean about the ones that weren't "crunchy"? Had I been buying mushy kosher dills all along without even knowing it? My undergraduate degree in semiotics wasn't doing a thing for me here.

Finally, I shoved some goddamn jar of pickles or other into my basket—bread and butter sandwich slices, probably, I was that overwrought—and rounded the last aisle into the produce department. Here I would pick up a bag of apples and a head of lettuce, then swing by to round up the boys in the bakery. I looked over automatically to check on them in their customary spot.

They were not there.

Puzzled, I pushed my cart to the front of the store, thinking they'd gotten tired of waiting and had come to the checkout to look for me. But they weren't there either. I stuck my head out the front door and checked the sidewalk, peered into the car. Nope.

It was probably right around then I started hyperventilating. I ducked back into the store and rushed to the information desk. "I can't find my kids," I told the employee.

Somebody began paging the boys over the intercom. Somebody began walking the aisles. Somebody went to check the bathroom. "No, ma'am," he reported, "they're not there." Somebody was calling 911. Concerned faces flashed past me as I ran back and forth past the checkouts, screaming "Hayes! Vince! Hayes! Vince!" in every direction. I rushed back out to the parking lot to call their names. But they were nowhere. My heart was pounding.

This is really happening, I was saying to myself. This—is—really—happening.

NO! I thought immediately. This isn't really happening. This can't happen. This definitely can't happen to me because I've already paid my dues, my life has already been pillaged by doom. In an instant, a whole debate about the concept of dues, the existence of karma, the notions of fairness and of evil went through my head. Don't think about it, I ordered myself. Don't think about the friend whose mother lost her husband and her baby in a three-week period. Don't think about the parents of those kindergarteners in Scotland. Don't think about Bosnia, about a woman being raped by the man who just decapitated her newborn before her eyes. Don't think of what can happen in this godforsaken place, the world. Don't think. Not yet.

Back in the store, I checked with the motherly lady at the bakery counter. "Why yes, sweetheart," she said, "your two little boys came by here to get their cookies. But that was, golly, maybe thirty minutes ago." Suddenly her expression seemed to harden. "Have you lost track of them?"

I pictured myself telling the cop, Yes, I let them go off by themselves. Yes, the last time I saw them was thirty minutes ago. No, I never told them not to talk to strangers. Suddenly our happy routine seemed like a reckless recipe for disaster. And then the horror movies started in my head. The quietness of the house. The phone calls I would have to make. (At least, I thought hysterically, I won't have to call their father.) A half-eaten bowl of cereal floating in milk on the kitchen table. Their sweatshirts, not yet folded in the laundry basket. NO. I would never go back to that house without them, I thought, never. I'd just walk out of the store and into the river.

Christ, where were they?

I started to shake, to cry. I felt my throat closing up, closing off the air, closing off my voice, and my heart pounding as if it would explode. Ten whole minutes had gone by. The first ten minutes of the rest of my life. Another shopper put her arm around me. "Now honey, the police will be here in a minute," she said. "And we can put up posters with their pictures on them."

POSTERS WITH THEIR PICTURES ON THEM? As if they were lost pets? This was supposed to comfort me? If I'd decked her right then, I'm sure a jury would have acquitted me. Just then I heard a voice.

"Ma'am. Ma'am. Here they are. They were in the bathroom all along. Don't know how we missed them the first time."

There they were, filthy T-shirts, battered knees, untied high-top sneakers, dirty blond hair, backwards baseball caps. All there. I dropped to my knees, hugging them, still shaking and crying, the relief taking a while to sink in. They're back. They're fine. Just another twenty-minute bathroom visit, that's all. Even at home I sometimes wonder where they've gone off to.

Meanwhile, they had no idea why this was such a big deal, why Mommy was acting like a mental case. "Mom," said Hayes, his brown eyes studying me with concern. "Get up, Mom. Calm down. Can we go wait in the car?"

"No, Hayes, you cannot go wait in the car. You stand right here next to me. You too, Vincie."

"But Mom, we weren't lost. And we tried to find you before we went to the bathroom, but Vincie couldn't wait anymore."

"I know, baby, I know," I said. "It's all right now. It's all right."

But seven hours later I could still feel the adrenaline coursing through my body. Today, I still get nauseous thinking about it, and sitting here typing these words my eyes fill again with tears. Yet after questioning them carefully—Would they go off with a stranger? Would they leave the store without me? Do they know how to have me paged if they can't find me?—I decided they really were old enough to handle this freedom. Since then, I've given them even more. They are allowed to cross the big street and go to 7-Eleven by themselves. They can stay home alone for a half-hour while I run to the store. I want them to be independent and I want them to be trustworthy—in the end, won't that keep them safer than overprotectiveness?

The joys of parenthood run side by side with its terrors: the twisted bicycle by the side of the road, the second when you can't see them at the beach, the news item you obsess on for days, the quick panic when you hear the school secretary's voice on the phone. One person's reasonable caution is another's paranoia and a third's unforgivable carelessness. And whenever something goes wrong, or seems to go wrong, you totally lose faith in your ability to make those distinctions.

I want to trust my kids and I want to trust the world. I hope I have the judgment to know the limits of that trust. I hope I never make any big mistakes. I hope—I pray—fate is kind to me if I do.

Okay, I admitted it. I pray. And I tell my kids to pray, too. For example, when Sparky the guinea pig disappeared from his cage on the front porch and that night the temperature went down below freezing, I told them to pray for him, to pray that he had been stolen—or "found"—by nice people who would give him a good home rather than by a hungry German shepherd or a family of Peruvians, who consider guinea pigs a toothsome entrée, and also rather than scuttling off on his little guinea pig legs into the now-frozen brush. We had looked everywhere. We had asked around and made a few phone calls. We had even put up posters with his picture on them. We didn't have a photo, so Vincie had to draw him—a black scribble with black eyes and black claws poking out. It was the best we could do.

All that was left was that act of last resort, prayer.

And while we were praying for Sparky, I put in a prayer of forgiveness for myself, since it was me who didn't put a top on the cage and me who resented cleaning it so much and me who considered Sparky's care and feeding such an unreasonable chore. And it doesn't take too much crazy quid pro quo, domino-effect reasoning to conclude that failure to adequately protect one's guinea pig leads ultimately to having one's children kidnapped in the grocery store. Left the top off the cage one time too many, didn't you? No! Please! Forgive me, Whoever/Whatever. I'm sorry, I swear!

It would be nice to believe in a nice, definable God, to have that sort of clear religious understanding to pass on to my sons. But I don't. There is too much evil and too much injustice and too much randomness for me to accept the idea that there is some sort of Overseer in control. Most aspects of the major religions of the world seem like fairy tales to me and I find it curious and even mind-boggling that people actually believe in them. For this reason, it doesn't seem right to bring my children up as Jews, though I consider both myself and them Jewish in an ethnic sense, and though I realize that this means that in order to rebel, they'll have to freak out and become Moonies or Hare Krishnas sometime in their teens. Hey, I did it. I spent two years chasing around after Baba Ram Dass, and papered the walls of my college dorm room with pictures of Shiva and Kali, in whom I actually, literally believed.

All that is left to me now of my early Judaism and Hinduism is a vague but stubborn faith in a "great spirit," perhaps the sum of all of our spirits. I also feel deep respect and reverence for the natural world, for its breathtaking intricacy, order and chaos. Somewhat quixotically, I also believe in prayer. Prayer is generally considered a religious activity, I know, and religious is one thing I am not. I am not a New Ager, either, though my revisionist, post-psychoanalytic approach to prayer will probably seem so to those who believe Jesus died for our sins.

But yes I do, I believe in prayer. Just as I have no idea what happens to our souls—if anything—after we die, I have no idea what happens to our prayers. Yet I pray all the time. I pray for strength. I pray to be a better person and a better mother. I pray that my many mistakes, my carelessness and my stupidity won't somehow ball up together and wreck my life.

Sometimes I pray out loud, at dinner, or in the kids' bedroom at night. "Thank you for our food," goes the little grace I made up when they were younger. "Thank you for our friends, and thank you for our family. Please keep us all healthy, and safe, and strong, and please bring food to all the hungry people in the world."

Who am I thanking? Who am I petitioning? I really don't know. But I know gratitude is important. And praying at night, as everyone knows, keeps the boogeyman away.

I tell my kids that when they feel they need their father, when they miss him really bad and wish they could talk to him, they should pray and maybe

Daddy's spirit will hear their prayers. I don't feel hypocritical about this. In my opinion, prayer works, at least in the sense of giving us an outlet for the fierce need to give voice to our unfulfillable yearnings—to speak to and with and against the mysteries that control our lives and take our loved ones away. And I certainly have no proof that Daddy's spirit *won't* hear their prayers. Or mine, for that matter, often addressed to him during my severest parenting breakdowns. *Tony, where are you, man? You have to help me.* So these prayers usually begin.

Because evil is everywhere, because we all make mistakes, because our hearts are so fragile and love is not enough to save any of us, I think we should all pray as often as we need to. Hayes and Vince should pray for Sparky's safety and I'll pray for theirs. I'll say this:

Please, please, let me keep them.

"Boys," I say, slowing the Jeep as I turn onto our street. "Do me a favor. Let's have a calm afternoon. Not like this morning. No fighting. Be nice to your brother, Hayes."

"I am nice. He's just so in-noying!"

"You are not nice!" Vince disagrees. "He's mean!"

"C'mon, guys. This is what I mean. Just say, 'Okay, Mom.'"

"Okay, Mom," they chorus obediently. I can't turn around, but can easily imagine the sincere expressions on their faces.

We pull up in front of the house, a light blue one-story box with deeper blue trim on the mismatched windows, its rectangular geometry softened by an encircling fringe of tall, thick, wild-looking nandina bushes. Two yellow rubber ducks perched atop a mound of other outgrown bath toys can be seen through one elongated glass pane. In three years of neglect, the steeply sloping front yard has gone from xeriscape to zeroscape—half overgrown, half dead. My husband was the gardener around here; when I

37

had to decide what to take care of after his death, only the children and the cat made the cut. The century plant and the coral yucca look all right, the purple sage and rosemary seem to thrive, and nothing will stop the nandina, but the rest of it is pretty much a trampled, weedy mess.

"Don't leave your Slim Jim wrappers in the car! Carry your backpacks! Don't forget to shut the car door!" I'm calling as the boys bound out of the back seat and up the concrete steps. Hayes stops to hook a finger under the rim of the empty blue recycling bin and haul it up to the porch—the first time I saw him make this gesture unbidden it was so casual and manly and considerate it brought tears to my eyes, and then the next time he didn't do it and that made me cry, too. He tosses it among the ice chests, milk crates, folding chairs, birdcages and political yard signs of yesteryear as his little brother bangs open the door, which sticks unless you kick the lower right corner in just the right place. They burst through the bright yellow foyer into the large wood-floored central area that is living room, dining room, kitchen, and family room. When I ripped down the walls that formerly divided the spaces, I imagined it would look something like a SoHo loft. Instead, I got an Upper West Side day care center.

While I wouldn't enter a contest or anything, at

least this part of the house is fairly neat, since straightening it up and sweeping are something I do instead of getting any work done and since throwing things away—including favorite toys and uncashed checks and miscellaneous papers I find on the floor that turn out to be very important artworks MOMMY! YOU THREW AWAY MY HAT I MADE IN MUSIC CLASS! THAT WAS MY MOST FAVORITE HAT I EVER MADE!—is one of my hobbies and especially since my beloved darling beautiful cleaning lady comes on Tuesdays and it is only Wednesday. ("Thank God," I say by way of greeting each week when she arrives with her pail and vacuum.)

"Homework first! Hayes, don't even go near that television. *Twenty-four Hour Sports News Update* will have to wait." I dump the leftovers out of their plastic Bart Simpson lunch boxes, rinse them, and leave them to dry in the drain rack—over which hang the venerable, if slightly rusty, Flipper and Get Smart models my sister and I carried in grade school thirty years ago.

"But I already did all my homework at school."

"Well, let me see it. And you still can't turn the TV on until Vince is finished."

"That's not fair!"

"Life isn't fair, Hayes. Let me see that homework of yours."

"I need help, Mommy," says Vince, pulling a crumpled worksheet out of his backpack.

"Sure, baby. Here, let me sharpen that pencil. What do you need help with?"

I flatten out the paper and read him a word problem about Jill taking out ten books from the library then returning two. He's supposed to illustrate it and write a number sentence to go with it.

"Mommy, can we have a freeze pop?" Hayes pours a pile of spelling and math papers onto the table for me to look at.

"First of all, you didn't put your name on this one. And you just had a Slim Jim and a cookie at the grocery store!"

"But Mom, I'm still hungry! I'm starving! When's dinner?"

"Oh my God. Dinner? It's not even four o'clock!"

"Mom, please, I'm really hungry. I'm not kidding, Mom." Hayes scrunches his face into a look of beseeching agony.

"Well—all right. Just one. First put your name on this thing."

"I want a popsicle, too," Vincie cries.

"Don't whine, Vince. You can have one as soon as you're done."

"That's not fair!"

"Nothing's fair, Vince. Didn't I just say that? Now let's get to work."

"I don't even know how to draw a book," Vincie mumbles dejectedly.

"Just draw a rectangle."

"But it won't look like a book."

"Well, it looks enough like a book. It's a math problem, not an art project. Hayes, put down that ball and put your name on this paper."

The phone rings. It is a magazine editor, calling about an article I've turned in.

"Hello. Wait. Oh, dear. IS IT REALLY POSSIBLE THAT YOU JUST TURNED ON THE TELEVISION, HAYES?"

"Mom, I'm missing my favorite show."

"Did you get the fax?" says the voice on the telephone.

The front door slams and Daniel Dominguez, the neighbor kid, walks in.

"Hi, Daniel!" says Hayes.

"My mom rented Sixty-four-Bit Nintendo," says Daniel. "Want to come over and play?"

"Mommy, I don't want to do this now," Vince wails.

"Hold everything," I say. "Barrie, I'm sorry. Talk to me."

"We had to cut quite a bit off the end of that piece you did for us—didn't you get the fax I sent you?"

"Excuse me, Barrie. WHAT ARE YOU DOING WITH THAT BASEBALL BAT, HAYES? Don't you think you've broken enough windows for one month?"

"Mom, I can't do this homework. You said you would help me!"

"You're an imbecile," Hayes scoffs.

"MOM! Hayes called me a embi-cile!"

"Let's go to my house!" urges Daniel.

"Good idea! Go, all of you, get out of here. No, wait, not you, Vince. We have to do this homework. Oh, lord. Barrie, I'll call you back."

"How come he got to go to Daniel's and I didn't?" Vincie's expression is horror-stricken.

"Because Mommy's going to help you do this sheet now, sweetie. Come on, let's draw those books." I lean close to Vince and watch him painstakingly draw ten rectangles, then cross out two with wiggly *X*'s.

"Eight!" he says triumphantly.

"Yes!"

We color triangles, divide squares in half, count pennies and dimes—and then it's done. He grabs his freeze pop and runs out the door and all of a sudden it is very, very quiet.

Things to do: Pick up room, which in twenty minutes has become a complete disaster area. Read fax. Empty dishwasher. Start dinner. Find shin guards and cleats for soccer practice. Listen to messages on answering machine. Return calls.

Right. Let's go.

Why can't I get up?

The door bangs open. "Mom," pants Hayes. "Where's the soccer ball?"

It works like a charm. I fly out of the chair, yank open the dishwasher, spread the fax on the counter, throw a pot on the stove.

"Do I look like Houdini? Do I have X-ray vision? Have you even looked for it? I saw it out by the mail-box yesterday. If you don't put your things away, how do you ever expect to find them?"

Hayes patiently waits out my spiel. "Could you help me, Mom?"

Isn't that what I'm here for? I wipe my hands on a towel and follow him out the door.

"How much you wanna bet I find that soccer ball in two seconds? Hey! Look! It's right here, Mr. Calls-His-Little-Brother-An-Imbecile! I can't believe you didn't fall over it coming in to ask me where it was!"

3

Our Bodies, Their Selves

There are days when the only reason I love my children is because they're so unbelievably good-looking. That honey-colored hair. The curve of that baby belly. The wholly innocent lower lip. Those round, clear eyes with their pale fringe of lashes. Sometimes a sweet little bare foot with a 101 Dalmatians Band-Aid on the fourth toe, can almost make up for two hours of whining and a puddle of Gatorade. I often answer the question "How are your boys?" with "They're adorable." Well, they are.

I love my children's bodies, and they love mine. (*They* don't think I'm fat, the little dears.) Of course we feel this way: we used to be one. In the beginning, they popped right out of me and amazed me with their loveliness, their soft hair, their tiny hands, their midnight blue eyes—and their fingertip-sized penises and swollen purple testicles, which to this day I have trouble believing were manufactured here in Marion's womb. As if their beauty alone might not be enough to win me over, there was the sheer physical delight of taking care of them, of cuddling and carrying and cradling, of relearning the parts of my own body in motherly terms. These breasts, these hips, this lap—now I get it! Equipment!

I was a passionate breast-feeder from day one. It enthralled me that my body had the power to sustain another life. Nursing was so clearly a sensual experience that I joked about how fast my infant sons could get my bra off, and speculated as to how my nursing unabashed in virtually every environment and position would play out in their post-pubescent futures. No matter how I joked, I never felt weird about it. I knew that you can't hold a baby too long, or kiss his toes too often. The fact that I enjoyed it so much was wired into me for the perpetuation of the species.

Oh, that seems like a long time ago. Though I still love to hug and kiss my big third grader and his younger brother, it's getting hard to believe I used to stick a breast in their mouths. And after years of bathing, dressing, and sleeping with them, and parading around the house in the nude (as I have been prone to do all my life), I'm starting to feel a little shy. As young as they are, the first green shoots of sexuality began to germinate in the little fellows some time ago, and I have to be careful about the role that my body—the Opposite Sex in its inaugural incarnation—plays in their development.

Our gradual loss of innocence seems to have begun as far back as the day I stopped nursing. When Hayes at eighteen months would tackle me, push up my shirt and storm my brassiere, often biting me with his new set of teeth, I began to feel sort of violated. I remembered the good old days when my breasts were my sole and private property: nonfunctional, eroticized, never on view to strangers in restaurants. Enough with the udders. I wanted my pointless breasts back. Yet while I was suddenly over nursing, I wasn't ready to relinquish the comfort we got from the touch of each other's skin.

Until Hayes was seven, we still took baths together, slipping and sliding around the soapy tub. At night, both of them would toddle, later tiptoe, into my bed, clinging like barnacles to the mamaboat until dawn. I had mixed feelings about this practice, as Vincie had the habit of wrapping his little hands around my neck, rhythmically clutching and unclutching, and Hayes would often wake me with a hot stream of pee. I put up with it for years nonetheless, while poor Tony pitched camp at the far edge of the bed.

Sometimes in the bathtub, one of them would point to my breasts and say, "This is where I used to get my milk."

"Right," I would say.

"Can I drink from your boobie now?" would be the next question.

"Nope," I would answer. "We don't do that anymore."

Occasionally this would be followed by the plaintive request, "Can I touch one?"

I considered a minute. "Sure, why not."

Then, in a couple of seconds: "Okay, that's enough. Let me wash your back."

Now those days, too, are over. It's happened in stages. The first was when I realized that even if it was okay to be naked around my kids, it might not be okay around somebody else's. This first occurred to me about three years ago, as I was standing dripping wet and stark naked in the kitchen, talking on the phone. I heard the front door open. Good news: it's the kids. Bad news: they've got two neighbors with them, ages six and eleven. Fortunately, it was a portable phone and I had time to flee.

When I got to the bedroom, my eyes fell on the two framed portraits of me hanging on the wall, given to me by a photographer friend who did a series of pictures of people without shirts on, hoping, I think, to make an anti-prurient statement by including all ages and sexes and races as subjects. In one of the two black-and-white photographs, I'm nine months pregnant with Vince, whalelike and dreamy, my arms crossed above my pendulous breasts with their big dark nipples pointing earthward. In the other, taken about two weeks after his birth, I am lying on my back beneath a small Mexican painting of Mary. My stomach is flat, my expression is troubled, and my breasts, engorged with milk, are the size of cantaloupes and almost as spherical. They look as if they're about to explode.

The reason I hung these pictures in the bedroom is so the UPS guy won't see them, and I try to remember to take them down when my in-laws are in town. That day, having narrowly escaped greeting Daniel and Joey in the nude, I realized that the boys and their friends might not get the anti-prurient thing either. But I haven't taken down the pictures yet. I'm waiting till the very last minute, which will be the first time I catch them in there on a little field trip with their buddies to ogle Hayes and Vince's mother's tits.

I walk the line, I know it, and am a total libertine compared to many parents. My sons have friends who won't change in front of other boys; I bet those kids' parents are never seen less than clothed. But I don't want us to be like that. I want my kids to know I'm not ashamed of my body and no one else should be, either. The idea that nakedness is something secret and embarrassing is one I just don't buy, and won't sell to them.

But then there was the night when Hayes about six and I was getting dressed for an evening out. He was in the bedroom with me, supervising. I held up dresses from the closet and let him choose; he watched me blow-dry my hair and do my makeup. Then just as I was slipping on my panty hose, he popped the question. "Can I touch your vagina?"

Well, durn, Hayes, as they say down here in Texas, I don't think so. In fact, I'm quite sure not. As innocent as the suggestion might have been on his part, the questions in my own mind would have tainted it. It had the feel of an experience he would remember, and brood about, and come to feel strange about later on. I, for one, felt strange right then and there.

Around this same time, I noticed Hayes and his friends starting to work out their interest in the human body among themselves. Girls were chasing the boys and boys chasing the girls on the playground; there was loose talk of crushes and who loved whom. In private moments, the ick! facade was dropped altogether and I witnessed a few sweet instances of tenderness and exploration. For example, shortly after the shower incident, we were flying up to New Jersey to see my mother, and Hayes noticed an adorable little girl in the row behind us. I wish I could have recorded what followed with a hidden camera: the opening scenes of *The Opposite Sex, Part Two.*

Within minutes, he had coerced the cutie pie into the seat beside him; I had been dismissed to sit beside her grandpa. My son was strutting his stuff—writing out the names of his family members and pets, then hers, describing in detail the many wonders of first grade. Most intriguing was their physical interaction: I saw him pat her shoulder, later caress her face, finally touch one of her teeth and ask if she knew its name. An incisor, he told her. What a pickup line. The six-year-old version of "You have such beautiful lips." A few minutes later, they were actually playing a game where one of them dropped a crumpled napkin down the back of the other's shirt, then reached in to get it as it fell out the bottom. Jesus, I thought. I hope the grandfather doesn't notice.

But I sure did. I noticed that Hayes was looking at girls. And once he started looking at girls, the rules changed for the somewhat overdeveloped girl he shares a bathroom with. I have had to learn the virtues of a strategically draped towel, perhaps a bathrobe, even—not that I owned one—a ladylike nightgown. I'm still no paragon of modesty, but I have started to feel uncomfortable on occasions when they catch a flash of maternal nudity and they flat-out stare.

As it turns out, the changes in them have coincided with a little sexual awakening of my own. I rarely saw myself as a sexual being during the years of pregnancy and nursing, which were followed closely by the years of my husband's illness, lacking in the bedroom department as well. Almost everything about my life was rated G, or maybe PG for profanity, for a long, long time. Even my vagina could barely rate an R, its life was so dull.

It is practically a cliché that death inspires sex, and I was no exception to this rule. Propelled by what I prefer to think of as life forces impossible to ignore, not far into my widowhood I acquired a boyfriend, some questionable lingerie, and a lock on my bedroom door. Suddenly, Hayes and Vince were not invited. Yes, it was sort of heartbreaking when we first shut them out and they stood there in the hall banging and crying, but as my boyfriend told me, just be firm for a couple of days and it'll be over. He was right. We don't even lock it anymore, and they sleep right through the night. As do his daughters, who come along for the night when he has them, and stay in the guest room down the hall.

Hayes continues to have great taste in women. Yesterday he invited an adorable and very bright little girl from his third grade class over after school, and he took her to 7-Eleven on the way home and bought her a Slurpee with his own money. When they got home, he sat her down on the couch and showed her his photo albums. His trip to Disney World. His summer vacation. Him and his dad.

They are so cute. It continues to slay me. It continues to make me catch my breath as if noticing for the first time. And—most important from an evolutionary perspective—it continues to make me keep loving them when I forget almost every other reason. Yes, it's different now. A bit more platonic, I suppose. And though I will always miss the easy physical intimacy we shared as mother and baby, I can see that our new kind of closeness, with its preliminary, awkward acknowledgement of the fact that we are opposite sexes, will be no less hard to surrender when the inexorable process of growing up changes everything again.

4

Good Sports

I have believed since earliest childhood that people who played team sports were from a different branch of the human species than I, one I regarded with a combination of jealousy and incomprehension that hardened later in life to disdain. And yet I, a prime specimen of Homo spaziens, a geek, a freak, the kind of kid who would have gnawed off her own arm to get out of gym class, have given birth to a young athlete. Yes, from these nonvarsity loins has sprung a fair-haired loose-limbed easygoing eight-year-old master of the universe, and he has led me to greener fields than I've ever known. So many years wasted on sex and drugs and rock and roll, when transcendence was waiting for me all along, in middle age, on the sidelines of a soccer field.

Perhaps you've already heard the earthshaking news: at 7:40 P.M. Central Time on November 22, 1996, the Black Knights trounced the Green Hornets to win the Under-Ten Division championship of the

West Austin Youth Association Soccer League. The final goal of the game—of the season, in fact—was made by my own number ten, who trapped a punt kicked upfield by a defensive back, dribbled it past several Hornet challengers, then bombed it over the goalie's outstretched fingers into the net.

This was number ten's first and only score of the season, and the sheer miracle of its having been made in the final minutes of the final hour amazed everyone, including the team's top scorer, tiny but deadly number seven, who leapt into his teammate's arms with glee. Several minutes later, the game ended, with Black Knights victorious and turning cartwheels on the field, champagne corks popping and the notoriously loud Black Knight parents more obnoxious than ever, beside themselves with joy, hugging and congratulating number ten's mother as if her son had just won the Nobel Prize.

At a post game event held at a local pizza joint, one gangly dad, sire of number three, the fearsome defensive sweeper, was heard to mutter hoarsely, "I was never on a winning sports team in my whole life. This is one of the great moments. They'll tell this story for the rest of their lives." Other parents compared the Knights' win to the Yanks' World Series triumph or the Cowboys' first Super Bowl. Kudos were heaped upon the Knights' devoted coach, a former city council member, while the mother of number ten sat in a euphoric daze, appreciating the appeal of sports for the first time in her uncoordinated life.

Just think of it: a black-and-white ball rotating through the floodlit air, sailing not too high, not too wide, not too late but just right, as if the laws of nature had opened a loophole for her son, or perhaps as if there really were such a thing as magic.

I'm really not any more athletic than I ever was, but the camaraderie of sports has sucked me in. Not so many years ago, I was driving through town on a Sunday in January and noticed that the streets were utterly empty. I mean deserted. It was as if the town had been evacuated and nobody had bothered to tell me. I stopped at a store to buy a newspaper and find out if we were due for flooding or a nuclear explosion.

"No, ma'am," the clerk told me, "it's Super Bowl Sunday."

"Oh," I said. So all over town people were gathered together eating potato chips and drinking beer, cheering and sighing, oohing and aahing, and I wasn't invited. I tried to feel superior, but somehow all I could manage was glum.

While my late husband wasn't much of a football fan, once we had children, our friendship circle changed. We no longer knew the kind of people who gave parties in discos at 3 A.M. Instead, we knew the kind of people who ate chicken wings at Super Bowl parties. So we went. Of course we didn't watch the game. We were the ones in the back of the room, inhaling the snacks and talking nonstop until the serious fans shushed us up.

Over the past two seasons, however, my relationship to the old pigskin has undergone a major transformation. I found myself watching football not just one Sunday but every Sunday. The college games on Saturdays. Even Monday nights, I learned, were part of the deal. Though at first I asked a million stupid questions, soon I was following the plays, yelping over penalties, questioning fourth-down strategy. When the quarterback got sacked, I no longer thought he'd been fired in midgame. When the announcer referred to Dallas's franchise players, I didn't imagine that the Cowboys ran fast-food outlets. Third and twenty-four? Big trouble. Not only was I familiar with the arcane terminology—talk to me about expansion teams!—I was actually able to make out the location of the ball on the field. I'd come a long way from the days when I was so clueless that what I saw on the TV was unintelligible, a street brawl in iridescent Spandex. (Actually, I always did like the Spandex.)

So what happened to me? What do you think? As

usual, I did it for a guy. A little guy, actually, the one I drive to school every morning and tuck into bed every night. Hayes had become so passionate about football in general and the Dallas Cowboys in particular that I couldn't help it—watching football was part of loving him, part of being in his world. First we were reading Troy Aikman biographies out loud at bedtime. Then turning to the sports section as soon as the newspaper arrived. Before I knew it, our weekends were planned around the televised games. Though Vincie, I must note, remains a stalwart artiste and sits at the kitchen table where he cannot see the set, doodling, rolling his eyes and complaining for the duration of the game. "How long is this going to last?" he groans halfway through the first quarter. "Two hundred million years?"

After decades as a chameleon girlfriend, changing my personality for each new boyfriend, being a chameleon mom is no problem for me. While this sort of flexibility is generally looked down upon, I'm certain I have it to thank for an interesting life. I've had flings with ice hockey, bike riding, volleyball, and folk dancing. During the years of my marriage, I never left the house during the Olympics, at the side of my figure skater husband, who had me memorize the names and backgrounds of every competitor in this country and others. I have become a vegetarian, a carnivore, a wine snob, and an antinuclear activist by turns. In addition to Russian history and filmmaking, I know a little about hairdressing, haute cuisine, cross-country hitchhiking, and the breeding of Labrador retrievers. I have been a devotee of blues, disco, rock and roll, folk, bluegrass, rap, and classical music, and have done my best with country-western and industrial-ambient-techno-house. Love can make anything happen, and for me the converse may be true as well: I don't know if I've ever done anything except for love.

However, no one but my own flesh and blood could have ever made me a football fan, because I was so profoundly antifootball all my life, I wouldn't never have even dated a football fan who might change me, because the fact that someone liked football made them an automatic cretin.

And now look at me. Spelling Dion "Deion" and Emmett "Emmitt." Pining for Jay Novacek, who was out one whole season and then retired. Arguing against the necessity of drug testing in professional sports. Such is the life of a Cowboys fan, and fan I am.

Yet another sport has intruded on my life thanks to these offspring of mine, and it is golf. And believe me, my hatred of football was really nothing compared to my feelings about golf, since golf more or less ruined my life. I grew up fifty yards from the ninth tee of the Hollywood Golf Club in West Deal, New Jersey, and it was my disgruntled view throughout my childhood that my parents spent more time at its clubhouse than at our house. They played golf all the time. Every weekend. Every day in the summer. And a single golf match, with its requisite postgame lunch and drinks, seemed to take from sunup to sunset. You've heard of football widows; my sister and I were golf orphans.

My father was a bad but persistent golfer whose handicap hovered in the twenties; my mother was several times Ladies Club champion, trading the title back and forth with her archrival, a woman known to us as Bobby Worm. Our house was filled with trophies, silver platters and ice buckets from her various triumphs. Surrounded by endless talk of double bogeys and sand traps, by countless Opens blaring from the TV set, I somehow failed to develop an interest in the sport. Quite the opposite. I despised golf.

At the few lessons and golf clinics my mother managed to drag me to in my youth, I demonstrated as little talent for it as I did for tennis, volleyball, gymnastics, kick the can or any other physical activity. My only forays onto the golf course in my teen years were made after dark, usually in the company of a beau and a six-pack. By the time I was in college, I could see that golf was not only responsible for my deprived childhood, it was a bourgeois elitist patriarchal capitalist ecologically incorrect pastime which I would never have a thing to do with.

Then—anarcho-feminist revolutionary that I am—I fell for a golfer. That very same boyfriend who put the hook on my bedroom door now has got me involved with the godforsaken sport of fat cats, Scotsmen and preppies. Only the mellowing of age could make it conceivable that I would look twice at a man who owns a set of clubs and a pair of shoes with cleats, but apparently the years have taken their toll because not only did I look twice, I fell in love. Due to my early conditioning, I was tolerant of Robb's long disappearances into the verdant bowels of the golf course. I made no objection to watching televised tournaments. I listened patiently to long descriptions of various holes and matches.

Then he and my mother ganged up on me and started steering the kids in the direction of the links. First it was the cute little putters and the electric cup that kicks the ball back, wrapped up under the tree for Christmas like a toy. Slide-click—whoosh. Slide-click—whoosh. When I heard the sound of the putting machine for the first time in twenty years, my head jerked around in shock. For a moment, I was back in my parents' living room in New Jersey, where a black plastic gadget just like this one was as much a part of the setup as chairs and end tables. I could almost smell the cigarettes and the miniature dachshund.

As soon as my mother left town after her holiday visit, the putters were converted to their obvious natural function—weapons. So of course I had to hide them in the closet.

But Hayes, it turned out, was really interested. He begged Robb to take him golfing on weekends, and one time he actually bogeyed a par three. That was good enough for my mother, who bestowed on him a bag and small set of clubs. (We told Vincie they were his clubs too, but I don't think he believed us.) Soon the illusion that my childhood had come back to haunt me was stronger than ever, with everybody around me talking pitching wedges and back nines, with the house vacated on weekend mornings like a barracks at reveille, as the golfers rushed off to make their tee times. But this time my attitude was different.

Was golf really so bad? A nice walk out there in the landscaping, a four-hour gossip session, a break from the phones and faxes and beeping alarms of daily life? That might be nice. I found my head turning toward those TV golf matches I had so long ignored. It was the sharp whoosh of the club and the satisfying thwack as it hit the ball that caught my attention. I found I had a deep desire to hit something and hear it crack like that.

Then, during a visit to my ancestral home on the ninth tee, I shocked my mother by asking if Hayes and I might take a lesson together at her club. She seemed to swallow many natural responses to this request before responding with a simple "Sure." And the next morning found us out on the practice tee, the very one where I'd hosted those teen debauches twenty years before.

Using my mother's seven iron, I practiced the stance and grip the pro showed me, trying to ignore the fact that my son was already hitting drives a few feet away. Years of osmosis had their effect; I sort of knew what to do. I wrapped my hands around the shaft of the club, straightened my feet, bent my head, and swung the club back and through. And though I whiffed my share, with a few corrections and suggestions from the pro, I heard a few of the resounding cracks I longed for.

"Well, you've got the clubhead speed," he told me, "like your mom. You've got potential."

Yeah, right, I thought cynically. Now with a couple of years of practice and few hundred dollars' worth of equipment, I could probably learn to play. I knew enough about golf to know that it's not a sport you can master, or even become a reasonable novice at, very quickly.

Back home in Austin, I pulled the same trick on Robb as I had on my mother. "Hey," I said one morning when we were sitting around my kitchen table, "is there a public driving range where we could go to hit some balls?" He looked at me with a kind of rapturous surprise, as if he were falling in love all over again.

At a casual, low-rent range on the north edge of town, we purchased buckets of balls for a few dollars each and rented a ladies' club for seventy-five cents. Out on the range, I ordered the boys not to watch me. I needn't have bothered. Hayes was getting pointers from Robb, who can send balls into outer space like the guys on TV. Vincie was collecting bottle tops in the parking lot.

The next day, we all went to a municipal pitch-and-putt course, where each hole is about a third as long as a standard one and clubs are available for rent. A real golfer can get on the green with a wedge, then putt into the hole, practicing the short game so critical to a decent score. For a beginner, this "baby course" offers the opportunity to skip past the boring lessons and hours on the driving range and go straight to the fun part, to actually feel like you're playing golf.

You've got your fairways and roughs, your water hazards, your little joys and frustrations. You get the fresh air, the conversation, the appetite and the suntan. You get triumphs like the one I had on the sixth hole, where my tee shot hit the edge of the green, and I actually putted in in three. I couldn't wait to call my mother and give her the blow-by-blow.

As I watched Hayes set up for a drive, his blond head bent, his body still, his young face a mask of concentration, as I heard the whoosh of his swing and the thwack of his hit, I had no doubt that the golf gene skips a generation. His score for the nine holes was ten strokes less than mine.

Vincie, meanwhile, had lost interest back on hole four and was lying on a bench dropping pebbles into a mud puddle. "Mom!" he shouted as we came near. "This is so boring! Take me home!"

So you have a child, and you think you're going to mold him and shape him. He's going to share your interests. You're going to take him under your wing and show him the way. Then you wake up one day and find yourself a soccer mom, a Cowboys fan, and a frigging golfer, for that matter. It's the offspring who's done all the molding and shaping here, and you, meanwhile, have turned into something you couldn't have imagined.

And by the way, does everyone give birth to their opposite? Are the members of my high school's cheerleading squad now home playing Life with overweight, nearsighted children who prefer *Jane Eyre* to fresh air and almost anything to exercise? That would be fair, don't you think? And speaking of fair, what about that antisportsman, Vince? What *does* he like, really? Or do second children only know what they don't like, what's already taken, and what isn't fair? I hope not. The wide world has a lot more than sports in it, I seem to recall, and I'm counting on Vince to drag me back to the wan and bloodshot life I loved so well.

5

Bad Mommy Days

One recent afternoon I brought our neighbor Daniel home from school to play with the boys. At about five, his father came by to pick him up. "Can Hayes and Vincie eat over?" Daniel asked excitedly.

Before I could speak, Dan senior said, "Sure. I'm going to barbecue a chicken."

"Yippee," cried the kids. "Can we, Mom, can we?"

"Well," I said, "I was going to make spaghetti and meatballs . . ."

"We want chicken!"

"Well," I sighed. "I guess—"

"Hey, I'll just take them with me now," said Dan, "and give you a little time off. Come on boys. We can play soccer while the fire gets hot."

"Okay," I said sadly, though no one seemed to notice my Eeyore-esque tone. As the children finished up their game and got ready to go, I was filled with a deep sense of being abandoned. I was going to be sitting alone in the house all evening, much as I had all day, while just two doors down my sons had rip-roaring fun and succulent poultry with another family. My children didn't love me, nor did they care for my spaghetti and meatballs. I felt the back of my neck bristle and my eyes well up at the same time, and I slammed the book I had been reading down on the coffee table.

"I wanted them to have dinner with me," I muttered petulantly as the happy soccer players rushed to the front door.

Dan turned to look at me quizzically. I had, after all, just said it was all right.

In that moment, I realized what was going on, recognized the hypersensitive, irritable, molehill-into-Mount Everest, edge-of-despair, nothing-and-no-one-can-please-me-now feeling I felt coursing through my body. What else could possibly make me feel angry, weepy, bloated, ugly, greasy, slothful, jittery, itchy and raw all at once, my eyes, nose, and breasts throbbing in hideous syncopation, my mental equilibrium buffeted by tidal waves of unasked-for emotions, snapping me like a wet towel against a wall?

I took a deep breath. "Don't mind me," I said, "I have PMS."

"Oh," Dan said. "Sorry." A look of fear crossed his face and he fled out the front door.

I believe I almost followed him out and hit him. When a person has PMS there is no right way to behave. But acknowledging this around the PMS sufferer will only drive her into a frenzy. Do not show your fear. There is really nothing more annoying to a PMS victim than the patent terror she inspires in men. Sometimes, for example, when I am in the grip of the madness, I think of calling my boyfriend to come to my aid. But even as I reach for the phone, the happy fantasy of his rushing over to comfort me somehow shades into the vision of his inexplicably irritating me and I'm ready to kill him before I even pick up the receiver.

I can't believe this is happening to me. I never had PMS before. Only in the last year or so have I succumbed to the madness, which I'm told is not uncommon for previously unaffected women as they reach their late thirties—so maybe it's biology and not just bad karma. Which I certainly could have built up all those years I didn't have PMS, didn't believe in PMS and actually made fun of people who said they had it. I thought they were wimps. I thought they were faking, or at least working it. At the time, all I knew of PMS was a couple of nights spent systematically eating everything in the refrigerator. Ha. I wish.

As I become more conversant with this bizarre phenomenon, this *Reader's Digest* condensed version of a personality disorder, I'm at least getting better at recognizing what's going on. Because what's really terrifying is when you don't know you have PMS and you seriously believe you have lost your mind. Not too long ago, I had a truly awful debacle with my children in the process of trying to get them off to school. Once I had pried Hayes out of the closet where he was hiding, he slid across the hardwood floor in his stocking feet and smacked his nose into the doorjamb of the bathroom across the hall. It immediately begin to swell; I burst into hysterical tears and threw myself on the couch wailing, I can't take this anymore. Of course at this point the children climbed obediently into the car and starting behaving like little angels.

For the next several hours, I was wracked by waves of guilt and despair, turning an ordinary accident into an indictment of myself as a parent and a person. I wrote an entry in my journal describing the incident in tones so melodramatic that it sounds like a scene out of *Mommie Dearest.* By noon, I had called a parenting therapist, my general practitioner, the elementary school counselor and my ob/gyn—I practically turned myself into Child Protective Services. It was one of the darkest mornings in my recent life.

Then, slowly, the lights began to come on. I

checked a calendar. Then quickly canceled all the appointments I'd set up, called off the social workers and got in bed with a cup of tea and a mystery.

Once these remedies seemed to have worked their soothing magic on me, I phoned an endocrinologist friend. I'm having trouble with PMS, I told him.

"What are your symptoms?" he asked mildly.

"WHAT ARE MY SYMPTOMS?" I shouted, my face suddenly crimson.

He sighed. "This is why I don't take PMS patients. They come storming into your office, eyes blazing, hair flying and well, they're sort of demanding."

"What do you mean, demanding?"

"Oh, you know, they say things like, If you don't help me, I'll murder my husband."

Well, at least I don't have to worry about that. No, the innocent victims of my monthly mania are my children. Which means that in addition to PMS I have to suffer from major attacks of suffocating guilt. For as everyone knows, mothers don't get to have moods. Not because you had a fight with your boyfriend, not because you backed the car into a tree, not because *The New Yorker* rejected your story for the forty-fifth time, and certainly not because you have PMS—no one, least of all yourself, is going to absolve you of poor mothering for any of these reasons.

I'm not trying to blame everything on hormones

or any other excuse. No, I have confronted the evil mother that lurks within and I wrestle with her regularly. I don't think it was so bad when the kids were helpless infants. But in the past few years, confronted with personalities and urges to control as strong as my own, I've definitely walked on the dark side. My struggle began in earnest at a barbecue we were invited to a few years ago, not long after Tony's death.

A party! Great! I packed up a container of potato salad and loaded the gang into the car. Hayes and Vince chattered happily in the back seat on the way. But as Vince climbed out of the car in front of our friends' house, he happened to notice his feet, or more precisely, what was on them—heavy-duty, Velcro-strapped Power-Lights sandals. I had brought back a pair for each of the boys as a gift from a trip. The weather had only just warmed up enough for sandals, so they still fell into that troublesome category: new shoes. From the horrified expression that crossed the face of my volatile, persnickety four-year-old as he viewed his footwear—did I say that? I meant to say "my adorable four-year-old"—I knew we were in trouble.

"I don't want these shoes. I want my sneakers," Vince announced.

"But these are your new sandals, and it's spring now," I replied cheerily.

"I *hate* these shoes."

"Remember, you wore them last weekend and you liked them just fine."

"Take me home so I can get my sneakers! I want to go home right now."

"Forget it, Vince. We're not driving all the way home. We're here. If you didn't want to wear them you should have said something before we left the house." I turned and walked up the path.

Vince followed me, his screams becoming louder and more insistent as we approached the backyard where the party was in progress. "You *never* let me wear the shoes I want. I hate these shoes. I hate this party. You *always* make us go to stupid parties. I want to go home. TAKE ME HOME!!!"

I attempted to greet my host and be introduced to some of the other guests while the tirade unleashed itself around me. "He's a little cranky," I offered apologetically, as if any sentient being could not figure this out. "How 'bout a root beer, Vincie?" I said to my hysterical little buddy, now red in the face with fury. "Want some chips?"

"NO! I want to go home. I hate these shoes!"

The other guests, predominantly young, childless musicians who doubtless identified with the rebellious child more than with his beleaguered mother, looked on in surprise and mild annoyance at the scene. "What's wrong with him?" one dreadlocked fellow asked.

"He doesn't like his shoes," I replied.

He looked down at the shoes in question and shook his head sympathetically. I had the feeling he was about to tell me the shoes were out of style.

"But look, they light up," I enthused desperately. "Walk over here and show him, Vince."

As Vince was too busy screaming to pay any attention, his brother filled in. But whether he did it on purpose or not, Hayes minced across the deck in such a way that the little lights in the heels failed to kindle. The other guests watched curiously.

Meanwhile, from the sidelines, Vincie pelted me with a small toy, which hit me at hip level. Enraged, I whirled around, grabbed his shoulders, caught myself right on the brink of something, and picked him up and carried him around to the front of the house for a quiet moment.

"Vincie," I began, sitting him up on the roof of a car so he would be still, and at eye level. I repeated myself on the topics of summer shoes versus winter shoes and the impossibility of our going home right now. I suggested every solution I could think of: Take off the shoes and go barefoot, sit in the car and wait, watch TV, have some barbecue, what about a yummy root beer, did you see Tim's Godzilla collection, Look! Some other little kids are coming to play! None of this did a thing to allay his yowling. Frustrated, I plunked him down on the ground and fled to the back of the house.

I had barely gotten a beer and found a chair to sit in when my tormentor tore around the corner and jumped into my lap. His red, screwed-up face inches from mine, he screamed with unabated fury.

And, for the first time, I slapped him.

For me, parenting is like dieting. Every day, I wake up filled with resolve and good intentions, perfection in view, and every day I somehow stray from the path. The difference is, with dieting I usually make it to lunch.

Let's get this much out of the way: I love these boys with my heart and soul, and I am not an irresponsible, violent or seriously disturbed person. I didn't do drugs while I was pregnant, I don't tie them up or beat them with coat hangers, and I never leave them alone in the house while I go on vacation. I serve them three meals a day, I read them stories at night, I kiss their boo-boos and answer their questions and buy them ice-cream cakes on their birthdays. I hug them and kiss them and goof around with them every chance I get.

"Oh, boys," I have sighed as I drive them to school after one more difficult morning, "I am so sorry I don't have more patience. I guess they must have run out at the factory before they filled me up. And it's very hard sometimes to be one person doing everything. Sometimes I need a little break and I just can't get it."

"It's okay," said Hayes, patting my shoulder, "you're a fun mom."

This took me so by surprise that I laughed with delight. "That's nice of you to say, Hayes. You're a mensch yourself."

Then I watch them get out of the car and start worrying again. Fun, maybe, but am I a good mom? This is the question I brood over in blacker moments. I have, as I just confessed, hit them. I have yelled, cursed, called them "stupid idiots" and worse, and am prone to wild threats. "If you don't stop, I'm going to have a nervous breakdown." "If you don't stop, I'm going to kill myself." "If you don't stop, I'm going to leave you right here by the side of the road." I am impatient, and I am sometimes selfish, too absorbed in my own pursuits to handle them gently. I often fail to make them brush their teeth and am even more slipshod about flossing.

I am inconsistent: Some days we can have a snack at 4 P.M., other days it's too close to dinner, and this inspires them to nag me endlessly just in case it's the former situation. I sometimes leave them with a babysitter when they don't want me to, and I have more than once let my irritation about some grown-up matter spill over into my dealings with them. And while I worry about the unpredictable—the bad driver, the malicious stranger, the deep water, the nasty germ—I have noticed that I am not as vigilant as some in my enforcement of the protocols that are supposed to avert these disasters. While I'm at it, I might as well mention my permissive attitudes about television and junk food, which qualify me as a bad parent in some circles as well.

Good mommy, bad mommy, good mommy, bad mommy: Which am I? We all live with these mythical creatures in our heads, the effortless nurturer who derives nothing but joy from child rearing, and her evil twin, the bitch mother from hell, selfish, bored, using her children mostly to aggrandize herself. I know I am neither of these, but that's not to say I'm not acquainted with them, that they don't sometimes bat me back and forth like a little white ball on the Ping-Pong table of parenting.

I want to be the perfect mother with the perfect children in the perfect world. Unfortunately, I, my children and the world fall off the mark with pre-dictable frequency, and sometimes this seems so discouraging that I let things go straight from perfect to outright terrible. In my own critical eyes, I become Bad Mommy. That makes me feel so awful, I'll do anything to be forgiven, even if it involves Play-Doh.

We all say things we wish we hadn't said and do things we wish we hadn't done, breaking our own rules about parenting. Because of how intensely we're involved with our children, and how much we expect from ourselves, these errors can feel much worse than they actually are. But sometimes you know you've reached the end of the line, the limit of what is excusable and tolerable, and you absolutely must find a different way.

That's not far from how I felt that day at the barbecue, when I saw the bright pink prints of my fingers on Vincie's slapped cheek and the shocked expression in his eyes. "You're not supposed to hit me!" he shouted tearfully, holding his hand to his face. "Now I'm gonna have brain damage!"

"Well, I doubt that, honey," I said, caught between tears and laughter. "But you're right that I'm not supposed to hit you. I'm not. And I'm sorry."

But, part of me thought, you're not supposed to drive me totally out of my mind. This isn't who I want to be, and to be honest, this isn't who I want you to be either. As these thoughts swirled through my head, I hugged my son tightly, rocking back and forth. I assumed the other partygoers were at this point debating whether to call the child welfare department, though I was too embarrassed to actually look up to see if they were watching.

Just as unexpectedly as it had begun, the incident was over. Minutes later, Vince had climbed down from my lap and was happily playing with his brother on the front porch. I was having a beer and visiting with friends. Everything was the way I wanted it to be in the first place, almost as if the ordeal had never happened. But it had. And while I don't believe Vincie will be scarred for life, I don't feel good about lashing out at him in anger. There I was, being Good Mommy, taking my kids with me to a party on a Saturday, nicely dressed, for once, with brand-new shoes. Suddenly, I turned into Bad Mommy, shouting and slapping a four-year-old.

It's not like I don't know what to do when I feel pushed to the brink. It's not like I never heard of Stop, relax, breathe, count to ten. So why didn't I do it? And why, for that matter, is Vincie such a butthead? Isn't that my fault too, because I spoil him and discipline him inconsistently? Members of the jury, I ask you! Is there any doubt in your minds that you are looking at a bad mommy?

There has got to be a way to get off this seesaw.

While our kids are growing up, we are growing too, building individual parenting styles from the disparate messages received from experts, friends, relatives, our own instincts and our kids themselves. And we are only human. Unrealistic expectations are self-defeating; becoming obsessed with guilt when things go awry, as they are bound to in such a difficult and long-term project, doesn't help anybody. You can't very well move on and act the way you'd like to while mired in unworthiness and hopelessness. And all the time you spend brooding and punishing yourself is more time when your best self is not there for your kids. If you don't watch it, you go from being mean mommy to being depressed mommy—not all that much better, from the kids' point of view.

Look, you have to tell yourself, it's not that you're a bad mommy. You're just having a bad mommy day. These things happen. So get over it. As Mary Kay Blakely has so wisely written in her book *American Mom*, "Since civilizing children takes the greater part of two decades—some twenty years of nonstop thinking, nurturing, teaching, coaxing, rewarding, forgiving, warning, punishing, sympathizing, apologizing, reminding, and repeating—I now understand that one wrong move is invariably followed by hundreds of opportunities to be wrong again."

I recently made up a bedtime story for my children. It goes like this. Two little boys are at the table eating their breakfast when they notice there's a fire-breathing dragon in the backyard. "Mommy!" they say. "There's a dragon in the backyard!"

"Stop fooling around! Eat your cereal, we're going to be late," their mother shouts without even looking. "Do you know how much I paid for that cereal? I'm not about to see it go to waste! Come on, you two! You don't even have your shoes and socks on. I'm turning off the TV!"

"But Mommy, he's breathing fire on the play fort!"

"Boys, have you brushed your teeth? When was the last time you brushed your teeth? You're going to have a million cavities! If your teeth don't fall out of your head first! Do you know how much dental work costs?"

"Mom, look! There really is a dragon and the play fort's on fire!"

It goes back and forth like this for a while, the mother ignoring what the boys have to say and yelling like a maniac (my performance as the mother is spine-tingling in its authenticity) until finally she looks out the window and sees that the play fort is in fact on fire. She calls 911 and screams into the phone, "Send the fire department right away! My play fort's on fire! Help, This is an emergency! Excuse me—

children, this does not mean you don't have to brush your teeth! Okay, are they on their way? For God's sake, hurry! Do you have any idea how much I paid for that play fort?"

I hope how hard my children laugh at this story means it's helping to give them a little perspective on their mother's failings. I'm buying time, I suppose, until I become a Better Mommy, until I get that breathing and relaxing and counting to ten stuff down.

What comes after four again?

BECAUSE 5:30 soccer practices and 6:30 soccer games have horned in on the family's evening meal every other day this week, tonight I am going all-out. We are having the beloved Yellow Dinner. The Yellow Dinner, as you may have guessed, is composed entirely of things that are golden in color, and is also characterized by a major convenience food component. Complementing the mouthwatering entree, oven-fried Shake'N Bake pork chops, are canned corn, bottled applesauce, boxed macaroni and cheese, and Poppin' Fresh rolls.

Presentation here is of the essence: each color-coordinated item must be ladled out in a neat circular blob that *does not touch anything else on the plate.* A person less experienced than I in catering to the appetites of youth might not realize that, just as a soufflé can be deflated at the last minute by a slammed door, hours of careful preparation can be irreparably spoiled by allowing disparate foods to mingle during serving. I've heard of a mother who boldly situates the broccoli on the shore of the ketchup, trying to dupe her children into green vegetable consumption when they lick it off. Such tactics would not pass muster here. Nor do lame excuses about everything combining in the stomach during digestion.

"Please, Mom, that's gross. I think I just lost my appetite."

Wherever my children picked up the phrase "I lost my appetite," I do not know. But it has become one of the banes of my existence. Dinner nightmare number 105: One kid starts talking about farting and pee-pee, everybody else joins in in a can-you-top-this manner, screeching with hilarity, until someone claims to have "lost their appetite" and immediately, everyone else follows suit. They've all lost their appetites! And they scrape back their chairs and run out the front door, leaving behind the huge servings of seconds they just ladled onto their plates.

But tonight is the Yellow Dinner, we are not having any guests, and perhaps we can navigate around the perilous straits of scatology and lost appetites. Guests can be trouble in so many ways, for of course it is incumbent on the gracious host to vociferously adopt any and all food dislikes expressed by a visiting friend.

I am in the home stretch, dumping the corn into a pot, when I hear the refrigerator door creaking open ever so slowly behind me.

"Close it," I say without turning around. "Dinner is in ten minutes. Less, even."

"Mom, I'm dyyy-ing."

"But you've been eating nonstop since I picked you up from school, Vince. I can't imagine how you're going to eat any dinner as it is."

He looks at me with eyes so wide you can see white all the way around the blue. "I will, Mama. I really will!"

"Listen, why don't you help me set the table. That'll get dinner out even faster."

"I don't want to set the table! Just one piece of cheese?"

"No."

"A pickle?"

"No."

"Please, please, please, please!"

Oh, good, we're into the word repetition portion of the evening. "No, no, no, no—"

"Okay, okay, okay, okay!" Vincie's little face is twisted into a caricature of fury: wrinkled brow, frowning lips, alligator tears trembling in the narrowed eyes, now squeezed to slits and practically emitting blue sparks.

"Calm down, poodle," I tell him. Do not ask why I call him poodle, or I will have to confess that it's short for "Vincent Valdric Voodle, the Poodle Noodle

Doodle," which, along with "Vincie La Voo," is the common form of address for this poor child in his own home. Though he has banned the singing of the famous theme song I composed for him when he was a baby:

> *My name is Vincie La Voo,*
> *and I am here to poo-poo*
> *I am coming to town and*
> *I am wearing a crown*
> *I can't even talk and*
> *I'm just learning to walk*
> *But I can boogie-woogie-woogie*
> *till the sun goes down.*
> *Vincie La Voo! Poo-poo!*
> *Vincie La Voo! Boo-hoo!*
> *Vincie La Voo! Woo-woo!*
> *Vince-a-lator, Vince-a-lator,*
> *Vince-a-lator, Vincie La Voo!*

Though he has forbidden the song—especially because it is most often sung by a diabolically giggling older brother—so far he hasn't insisted that I stop calling him Poodle, or its many variants, such as Poodley-Noo and Poo-tell. I do not know why I do this. I do not know why I started calling the neighbor kid, Daniel Dominguez, Doogie Howser. I've never even watched *Doogie Howser.* And I don't know why I persist in my controversial career as a composer, driven to create musical works such as "Hayes-n, Amazin' Raisin, King of the Wild Frontier," despite the popular outcry inspired by my oeuvre.

I do know I am not the only parent who suffers from compulsive nickname behavior. Among my acquaintance are numbered children called Bij, Cakey, Goo-goo, Bug, Boogah, Cootie, Jodgie and Beaner. My own sister has admitted to referring to her child as Pumpkin Pie with Whipped Cream on Top.

Anyway, my kids have been known to call me You Big Stupid Lady and Poopoo Mama, so we're even.

It is a race to the finish line as the Raisin scarfs macaroni and cheese out of the serving bowl and the Poodle sticks his finger in the applesauce. It's Mom's Dinner Challenge: Can she get it on the table before they eat it all? I whisk the bowls off the counter and onto the table, which features two normal place settings and, at a third seat, the grown-up version of the Yellow Dinner—a single glass of chardonnay.

"Mom, how come you're not eating anything?" Hayes asks solicitously, fork poised over his pork chop.

Me, eat this shit? No way. I may not be macrobiotic or even vegetarian anymore, but I have not tumbled all the way to Shake'N Bake pork chops, or just about anything else the kids will eat: the canned chili and tamale dinner, the buttered noodles with parmesan cheese dinner, the grilled cheese and canned soup dinner, the fun-with-ramen dinner, the Hamburger Helper dinner or its many cousins, all lined up in clever little boxes in my pantry. And there's always the unidentifiable Crunchy Tan Thing, that ready-to-microwave nugget which forms the centerpiece of so many meals at home and out. Is it chicken? Fish? Mushroom? Egg roll? Pizza bite? Who can say?

Actually, I take it back, I kind of like the ramen.

The truth is, a lot of this food is exactly what I grew up on, then turned up my nose at when I left home and began my life as a bohemian artiste.

"I'm not that hungry," I tell Hayes, "I'll eat something later."

Yeah, right, like all the food Vincie leaves on his plate and everything remaining in the serving bowls, too. In this way, as every red-blooded American woman knows, I will not really be eating the food, and therefore it will have no calories, fat or cholesterol.

"Have something, Mom. Have the macaroni and cheese. That's one from grains and cereals *and* one from the milk group!"

Well, I think that may be overstating the case for

this particular rendition of the dish, but I don't want to give the kid a complex. "Oh, no dear, don't mind me, I don't need anything. *You* eat." When did I turn into such a Jewish mother? Shake'N Bake pork chops notwithstanding, I've really got this thing down.

I put a little corn on a saucer.

"Mommy, we forgot to say grace," Vincie informs me with his mouth full.

"Okay, good idea, go ahead and say it."

Together, they say the grace they learned from Robb's daughters, which they prefer to Mommy's homemade one, spilling the words out as quickly as possible: "Thank you for the food we eat, thank you for the world so sweet, thank you for the birds that sing, thank you God for everything."

"Amen," I agree.

Hayes finishes vacuuming round one off his plate and goes for seconds, while Vincie nibbles a tiny cube of pork chop and plays with his applesauce and lists the people he plans to invite to his birthday party, which is now only seven months away. "Sam, Daniel, Calvin, Caleb, Cody, Jasper, J.J., Jack, Marshall, Gabe—"

"Hey, you're not getting very far with that dinner," I interrupt.

He looks at his plate in dismay. "I'm stuff-ted," he reports.

"What a surprise," I say, mostly to myself.

"Can we go out and play now?"

"Take your plates to the dishwasher first. Actually, Vince, I'll take care of yours . . . And hey—don't go past the big lot! Are you wearing your watch, Hayes? Come back by seven-thirty—Bye!"

6

Books and the Night

Among the many aspects of parenthood I romanticized prior to having the experience myself was reading bedtime stories. I imagined myself passing my love for literature on to my little ones in the glow of a bedside lamp, sharing old favorites like *Good Night Moon* and *Madeline*. These were the stories my mother read me as child, and I remembered them with great fondness. They were the first episodes in a lifelong romance with books, one instigated by my mother, a woman who reads so voraciously it might be said she has a "reading problem." I believe the township council in her hamlet in New Jersey is considering reducing traffic by putting in a monorail between her house and the public library. "What's Mom up to these days?" I ask my sister, who lives near her.

"The usual," she confirms grimly.

"Grisham?"

"Yep."

Alas, by the time Hayes was five and Vincie three, I was completely disillusioned with bedtime reading. I had been through *Good Night Moon* several hundred times. I knew where the mouse was hiding, they knew where the mouse was hiding, and somehow I just couldn't bring much enthusiasm to the task anymore. Couldn't the mouse, for once, hide someplace else? Is there perhaps a point at which you've read it so many times you get brain damage and suddenly it's new to you again? Now where is that darn little mousie? He was here just a minute ago.

I think most parents of small children will agree: reading bedtime stories to young children is very often very boring. Half the time I would fall asleep before the kids did, leaving them to climb out of bed, chew five packs of gum and strew the house with Styrofoam packing peanuts. After a while, my disaffection got out of control, leading to all kinds of desperate ruses.

Since I couldn't do much about the inexorable content of our reading material, I began to goof around with my performance. I eschewed the standard read-aloud voice, the voice atremble with sincerity and enthusiasm, the voice auditioning to be the successor to Mr. Rogers. Instead, if only to increase my chances of remaining conscious when reading *Madeline* for the thousandth time, I began to experiment with different styles.

I would pretend I was a poet, reading to an audience of literati, complete with portentous line breaks and sonorous intonation. Think "Twelve Little Girls in Paris" by Galway Kinnell. Other evenings, I resorted to poorly rendered foreign accents. The sometimes oddly translated Babar books seemed to beg for Maurice Chevalier. *Story Time for 3 Year Olds,* a volume from the British Isles, got Julie Andrews on nitrous oxide, while *Hansel and Gretel* was delivered by Marlene Dietrich. (Dat vitch. Vat a bitch.) And by the way, was this story really meant to put kids to sleep? "Now fill the cauldron with water so I can boil your brother"?

Talk about Sturm und Drang. I much preferred the Zen-like simplicity of *Go Dog Go.* I haven't read it for years now, but still know it by heart. The dogs, their cars, the traffic lights they must obey, and of course, the romantic subplot in which bad fashion choices almost keep a pair of lovers apart ("Do you like my hat?" "No, I do not like that hat!") and finally, the grand climax of all this driving and accessorizing: the dog party in a tree!

Doesn't this book really say it all? Isn't so much of life, in the end, about big dogs and little dogs? About black dogs and white dogs? About being attuned to the greenness of the light, about knowing when to "go"? And the dog party in the tree—is this not a reminder that heaven is, after all, here on earth?

I'm sorry, this is what bedtime stories have done to me. At one point, I had gotten very bad indeed, trying to jack up the soporific effect of my recitation by reading the story of spunky little Fievel in a monotone or a barely audible mumble, by trying to get away with increasingly abridged versions of *Berenstain Bears on the Moon*. It became a contest to see how many pages I could skip without their noticing, how fast I could get those bears back to earth so we could all utter their timeless comments in unison. "Wow," they say—and we chime in fervently—"That was quite a trip."

I was just about at the breaking point. I might have ended up like my boyfriend. His daughters report that, by the end of their bedtime story days, he was invariably responding to a request for a tale with the following: "Once upon a time there were three bricks. A Mama brick. A Papa brick. And a baby brick. The End." But fortunately I came up with other solutions.

Weekly trips to the public library definitely improved the situation; we could forgo our dear old favorites more easily if we had something new for a limited time only. And by the time Vincie hit kindergarten, we were ready for chapter books. Boy, did I breathe a sigh of relief then. Ready to make the dear acquaintance of Henry Huggins, Ramona and

Beezus. Of Tom and Huck. Of Charlie, Veruca Salt and Augustus Gloop. I was beside myself with joy reading *Harriet the Spy* (I think I almost appreciate Louise Fitzhugh more now than I did as a child—she is just vicious on Harriet's Upper East Side parents) and looked forward as much as they did to our slow nightly progress through an illustrated edition of Louisa May Alcott's *Little Men*. The reports therein of life 150 years ago raised endless interesting questions: How did they travel if they didn't have airplanes? How could they have chess sets if there wasn't any plastic? And why did they have such long hair and get so dressed up all the time?

Well, anything's better than *Goosebumps,* a profoundly stupid series of horror-mystery books for youth in which every chapter ends with the plot jumping on your chest to take away your breath, and in which the mystery is very often solved by some illogical deus ex machina from the center of the earth or outer space. Of course the boys don't seem to agree with me on this, and are desperately trying to collect all two million of the idiotic things, though Vince and his friends are more interested in the covers than the content.

When Hayes really wants to drive me crazy, he knows just what to say: "I hate to read, Mom."

Don't tell me that, Hayes, I'll die.

It's time for some of my famous threats: People who don't like to read have miserable lives! They are bored out of their mind in the doctor's waiting room! Plane flights are hell! They sound like morons because they have minuscule vocabularies! They never find out what really happened, only the movie version! They are missing out on the greatest pleasure of life!

"Oh," says Hayes drily. "I still hate it."

Then I catch him reading Shel Silverstein poems in the bathroom or sneaking ahead in *Little Men*.

"Mom, what's a quadruped?"

When they are bathed and brushed and flossed and pajamaed and read to and night-lighted and kissed, the hundred-yard dash of evening parenting is finally over. For a few more minutes, I hear their whispered voices, then silence. I breathe a sigh of exhaustion and relief. One of my favorite parts of the day is finally here. I put on my nightgown, pour a glass of wine or a cup of tea, turn on my lamp, and get in bed with my book.

I read for half an hour, an hour, even more. I read until the moment when a heady, irresistible exhaustion overtakes me and after several attempts to keep my eyelids from fluttering closed, to keep the book held upright on my chest, I know it really is time to go to sleep—even though the heroine may well be pregnant, even though the hero is hot on the trail of the killer, even though the hurricane is about to hit the defenseless island. I check—ten pages to go in this chapter. I glance over at the alarm clock—oh, Lord, only five hours until it rings.

And so I reluctantly leave the world of the book I am reading—the cocktail party of the Russian nobility, the piney backwoods of rural east Texas, the campus of a snooty women's college in the 1940s—and find myself back in my bed, the covers warm and heavy, muscles so relaxed I have to move my legs just to see where they are. Beyond the golden circle of the lamplight, the house is silent and dark, the world beyond is silent and dark, and I affectionately place the book on the bed beside me, facedown against the quilt, open to my page, my glasses perched atop it like some long-legged, wide-eyed mantis, and I click off the light. We sleep together, me and my book, me and those characters, me and my mixed-up dreams.

The last time my mother babysat for me, I got home from my date to find the house dark except for two small lights. One came from the boys' room, where I discovered Hayes holed up under the covers with *Goosebumps* number forty-one (He never listens to me about anything! Anyway, I thought he hated to read!) and a flashlight.

"Go to sleep," I told him firmly.

"Aw, Mom," he complained, rolling away from me, almost asleep before his cheek touched the pillow.

At the other end of the house, Nana had already dozed off with Pat Conroy, and I gently slipped off her glasses and extricated the thick acetate-covered library book from her grasp, as I have so many times, and she woke up just enough to ask for a good-night kiss.

Somewhere in the middle of them is me, a stack of books beside my bed, their titles and subjects saying as much about me as any other collection of objects in my life. Instead of arranging them into the traditional categories—fiction and nonfiction, novel and short story, self-improvement and pleasure—bedside books are better divided into those that put you to sleep and those that keep you awake. Both have their place. Just last night I picked up a slender but densely written volume of literary criticism for the knockout punch I knew it would deliver should I peruse even a few sentences about images of the apocalypse in modern fiction. Sometimes just a single name—Alain Robbe-Grillet, for example—does the trick.

There are few pleasures as harmlessly decadent and readily available to the young, the old, and the single—whose lamps burning into the night bother no one—than reading a totally absorbing book in bed.

As the story overtakes you, as you flip the pages ever more urgently, as the world of the book becomes more real than that shadow world outside the lamplight, beyond the ticking clock, you find an escape more complete than almost any other, one that readies you for the plunge into sleep, where that most mysterious and accomplished storyteller, the subconscious, narrates the darkling world of dreams.

Even though I know that Hayes doesn't actually hate books, and that Vincie is on his way to becoming a reader, it does concern me that neither of them has taken to it the way I did. I think it's partly because they're boys and as such, are hormone-bound to stay in constant motion and make lots of noise the majority of their waking hours. They almost can't sit still— unless hypnotized by electronics. In the presence of moving images on a screen, they practically turn into furniture, attached to the computer as if they were just another peripheral, posed like mannequins in a toy-store display of Nintendo (look, the thumbs really move!), thrown to the floor and left there stunned by the Cartoon Neck-Work, as Vince believes this cable television channel is called.

I have counted how many times I have to say their names to get them to respond when they are watching television or playing video games, and have gotten as high as twenty-six. I just hope I never need emergency medical assistance during *Rug Rats*.

When Nana, that salesman of literature, comes down to visit, she'll have none of this. They are allowed to watch *Jeopardy* with her from five to five-thirty and that should be enough TV for anyone. Then she has Hayes read his library selection, *Fun with Soccer*, out loud (my reaction was, "Hayes, bring home a real book next time.") She does *Cat in the Hat* with Vince long past the point I would have passed out from frustration, but until he finally begins to see the difference between a *b* and a *d*. And it worked—right now, he's into the easy-reader version of the *Star Wars* trilogy, where you don't get very far if you can't read the word "droid."

If I had little girls, it would be different. Yes, it would be. Remember back in the seventies, when we all thought there was no innate difference between the sexes? It was all socialization and environment. So if little girls played with trucks and little boys were given Barbies, we confidently hypothesized, in no time our race would be virtually androgynous!

Oh, yeah, right. Now that most of seventies feminists have grown up and become mothers or aunties or at least next-door neighbors, we can only snort at this once-dear notion. Certainly neither sex is smarter or more capable in an overall sense, but they are definitely different. Even if you give them gender-bias-free toys, even if they have non-sexist parents who both work, even if their parents are lesbians or gay men, by the age of seven or eight, you will notice the following tendencies:

Girls are interested in people, feelings, and relationships. Boys are interested in noise, motion, and action. Girls will actually ask you a question like "Are Mike and Ellen married?" or "Is that guy with John's dad his friend or his boyfriend?" whereas boys will not even look up when Mike, Ellen, John's dad and his friend come into the room. Girls like to play pretend games that have romantic, sexual, or economic overtones. Boys like to play war.

I was discussing these matters over lunch the other day with a friend of mine who has three daughters, and together we came to this conclusion: Girls are bitches, boys are assholes. Put a group of girls together unsupervised and they will talk about everyone they know and tear them to shreds. Put a group of boys together and they will make an ungodly racket and break things.

And I say, *vive la différence*. Especially now that I've got two little girls in my life to read books and gossip with.

7

The Girls

Two hot Texas summers ago, my boyfriend Robb and I took all four of our kids—his daughters, my sons, all under ten at the time—on a ten-day trip to Canada. When people hear about this, their usual reaction is a combination of awe and horror. "No, really, it was wonderful," I assure them. "Just look at the pictures."

The one I display in my living room was taken by the ship's photographer on the HMS *Britannia,* which offers daily excursions up the coast from Vancouver. The six of us stand at the prow in order from tallest to smallest, the red-and-white maple-leaf flag blowing in the blue sky behind us. First is Robb, big and Irish-looking, with a mustache and a thick sweater. Leaning against him, I look unusually diminutive and feminine, my face framed by dark hair and the sleeves of a sweatshirt tied around my shoulders. Next come the kids: Katie, then nine, with her shiny bob and wide, serious eyes, then the seven-year-olds, Hayes and Julie, both wearing their last two meals on the front of their T-shirts. At the front is young Vincent, aged four and eleven-twelfths, looking like a little blond rapper in his oversized T-shirt and high-top sneakers. Aren't we cute? Almost like the Brady Bunch. Almost like a family.

Almost. After dating for three years, we aren't married or even living together. Those sorts of major decisions seem incredibly complicated. Unlike the Bradys, who sprang fully formed from the heads of their television creators, we have a past. In fact, we have pasts, plural. We have baggage, we have battle scars, we have former spouses, custody arrangements and financial issues. We have complex allegiances and unfinished business. We have grief and fear.

And we have kids. So while most romantic relationships are directed by the confluence of two opinions, in our case everybody gets into the act. The boys rush out of school and ask, "Are we getting together with the Walshes tonight?" After a group dinner, there is a general caucus over whether we should have a sleepover, or a "special exception," as weekday overnights are called. When Robb sleeps at my place, the girls sleep over too; when I'm in his water bed, the boys are down the hall in their nightshirts. When we go out, we get one sitter for all of them. "Get Mitzi!" the girls suggest. "No, Isaac!" counter the boys.

The larger questions, too, are widely debated. Several years ago, then-six-year-old Julie was the first to broach the subject of marriage. In the middle of our first weekend trip to the Texas coast, she took Robb aside to ask him, "You're not going to get married, are you? Marion's nice and all, but I don't want a stepmother."

Well, I wasn't ready to walk down the aisle either. "Don't worry, Julie," I told her after her dad reported the incident. "I'm not going to be your stepmother. I'm just going to be your friend."

One afternoon during that trip to Canada, I took big sister Katie out for high tea at a fancy hotel. Leaving the boys and Julie to their usual unruly pursuits, we donned patent leather shoes, hair bows and just a touch of lipstick for our outing. Upon making our grand entrance into the tearoom, we settled into upholstered club chairs and sipped Earl Grey from porcelain cups, pretending we were princesses, then when that got old, psychoanalyzing everyone we know.

We were talking and giggling over our cucumber sandwiches, making facetious suggestions about what she should get her dad for Father's Day—a live-in maid! a golf cart!—when suddenly Katie got quiet.

Her wide brown eyes full of earnest concern, she said, "My daddy would be as lost as a grain of sand without you, Marion."

I was so touched I couldn't speak, and my eyes filled with tears. What an amazing little girl. Some days, I think I'd be pretty lost without *her*.

When you think of it, since Robb and I began seeing each other, our families have been essentially dating en masse. Considering that this involvement created nine separate one-on-one relationships, and that a group of children of these ages and sexes doesn't necessarily coalesce as smoothly as this one has, we're very lucky. In fact, we are only half joking when we tell skeptics the kids get along better than we do.

The most complicated relationships among this minivan-full of people are those between the grown-ups and the children who aren't theirs: Robb and my boys, me and his girls. The trials of stepparents are well known; the emotional politics of unmarried significant others may be even trickier. With no formal relationship to the kids, their loyalty, love and authority are vulnerable to question.

And rightly so, in some cases. For while playing favorites among one's own children is not nice, socially acceptable or wise (and the fact that such preferences exist anyway is one of the basic unfairnesses of this unfair life of ours), things are different when they're not yours. Most parents bend over backwards to conceal partiality they feel among their own children, but the rules are looser with respect to other people's broods. When falling in love with kids you're not related to, you're not obligated to be absolutely egalitarian, dealing out your affections like hands of cards.

Katie is unquestionably the daughter I would have ordered if I had chosen from a catalog. A bookish, intuitive girl with long, thick eyelashes, a quick wit, and dreams of becoming a writer, Katie recognized in me a mentor just as I saw in her a protegée. While I'd been content for years with my young ruffians, suddenly I realized what I'd been missing. Someone to buy hairbands and locking diaries and *Nancy Drew* books for! Someone to take to high tea! Not to mention someone to help around the house, to spell me reading bedtime stories and loading the dishwasher. To notice when I am sad or stressed out, and actually ask why. Even the fact that Katie is a little uncoordinated makes me feel all the more like she's my own. From the day I met her, I was a goner, and missed no chance to catalog her charms.

"And Julie's adorable too," I would quickly add

at the end of my story. Julie is a blue-eyed, apple-cheeked, hip-swishing charmer with a clear soprano voice and a sunny disposition: her mother's daughter both in looks and in loyalty. Perhaps this is why, from the start, the two of us had a little less room in our hearts for each other than Katie and I did.

I love Julie—of course I love her! She's incredibly sweet and warm-hearted, kind to animals, friendly to strangers, quick to bond. A classic Julie story is that during a three-mile fund-raising walk for AIDS we all went on last year, she got sick of walking after about six blocks. The whole rest of the route, we kept seeing this sixty-pound second grader riding on shoulders of various good-looking strangers, getting pulled in wagons, and being revived with extra granola bars and Gatorade by doting surrogate mothers, smiling and gabbing animatedly all the while. As Katie commented, rolling her eyes, "I bet she's telling her whole life story again." And let me tell you, she tells it with drama and flair. "My parents are divorced," it begins, "so I only get to live with my dog part of the time . . ."

It's easy to make fun of Julie. Too easy, in fact. Because while I can call my own sons "terrorists" or "idiots" with total impunity, while I can tell stories of their misbehavior without anyone doubting for a minute that I adore them, my affections for Julie don't have the same quality of incontestability. A while back, her father told me he thought I was coming down awfully hard on Julie for being cutsie-wootsie— a little baby-talk girly-poo act she puts on that drives me nuts. I had to wonder if he was right. I try very hard to be fair, and part of the problem may simply be that I'm more inured to boy-style irritating behavior (usually involving mindless destruction of home furnishings or endless conversations about buttholes and peepee) than girl-style.

In truth, I thought I was treating her the way I would if she were my own—but if you give the scolding without the unconditional love, that's not right. I was worried about my relationship with Julie. Did she know I love her?

As it turns out, she knows far more than that.

On a trip to the coast this past Thanksgiving, I was caught off guard when the subject of marriage came up again. After the football game ended and the fans relinquished the TV set, the kids watched a movie, a remake of the genie-in-a-bottle story with Shaquille O'Neal. When it was over, I pulled out the crayons and asked them to draw pictures of how they would use three wishes.

Vincie drew a remote control car, a Hot Wheels

set, and on the third sheet wrote simply, "I wish I could have my birthday." Hayes was more grandiose: he listed a football field, a soccer field, a golf course, a tennis court, a basketball court, a volleyball net and a baseball diamond as one conglomerated Sports Wish, then went on to request a convertible and a million dollars.

Julie watched me closely as I flipped through her pile. She had wished for a bike light and a swimming pool; the last page stopped me in my tracks. It showed a couple hugging, with a woman standing off to the side shaking her fist. Across the bottom was lettered "That Mom and Dad never divorced but Marion was our closest friend." "Oh Robb," said the balloon coming out of her mother's mouth, and "I'll never leave you" was printed inside her father's. Across the page, the Marion cartoon was saying "What am I, cooked liver?" Not even chopped, but cooked.

Perhaps I should have felt disappointed that I'd failed to win her over after all this time. Instead, I burst out laughing. I was proud that she felt comfortable enough to admit her holdout status, her undimmed longing for her parents to be together, while offering me the rank of best friend as consolation. Heavens, I thought, she feels about the same way about me that I feel about her. And struggles with it, too.

Both for its intentional and its unintentional qualities, I loved the cooked liver, the way she'd cracked a joke to make her difficult truth easier to share. So I told her all that. And she replied matter-of-factly, "But I got it from you. You're our funny friend," at which point I took her in my arms and hugged her as hard I could.

Katie, who had waited patiently all this time, suddenly seemed ultra-eager for me to look at her drawings. She had wished for world peace, for her dad to quit smoking, and—beneath caricatures of Robb and me as bride and groom—"That Dad and Marion Got Together." I gave her a suspicious look. "I didn't even *see* Julie's drawing," she protested.

That night, I loved the girl who doesn't quite want me around as much as I do the one who's taken me into her heart. I hope Julie and I will be each other's cooked liver for years to come.

7:00 P.M.

WAS IT ONLY THIRTY MINUTES ago they went out to play? It seems longer. I've finished the dishes, wiped the table, flipped through the paper, gotten rid of two telephone solicitors and a market researcher. These days, I don't even let them launch into their pitch, because I'm afraid I won't be able to say no once I hear what it is. The blind citizens of Texas, the firefighters, the AIDS lobby, not to mention a bewildering number of carpet shampooers and one very persistent air-duct cleaning service (do I even have air ducts? please, don't tell me)—they've all got my number, probably on some special list of hopeless pushovers. But no more. Now, as soon as they ask for Mrs. Winky or request to speak with my dead husband, I say, "Whatever it is you want, you really must find some other way to ask me for it. Bye!"

But now it's pin-drop quiet here, and I kind of wish I'd stayed on the line, at least with the market researcher, who only wanted to explore my feelings about convenience stores. When the kids are home, the house often feels so overloaded and frantic that I can almost hear the ends of my nerves frying. A maelstrom of obnoxious noise swirls through our not-very-spacious floor plan—computer-game sound effects, cartoons, the all-hit radio station, the blood-curdling screams of sibling warfare, the ordinary stomping and shouting of boys having fun. As it tears along, it picks up any loose objects in its path—wet bathing suits, trading cards, abandoned sneakers, balls, pieces of a plastic Starship Enterprise model—whirls them around, and deposits them randomly around the house. And sucks me so deep into the insanity that I go from making relatively calm (and inevitably ignored) requests like "Kids, go on outside now" and "C'mon, y'all, skedaddle," to hysterical screams of "Get out of here! Get out of here! JUST GET OUT!"

And then they do. They are gone. The last flying sneaker hits the floor with a rubbery thud, and the vortex is now one of emptiness and silence.

What will I do in ten years when they leave for good? (Spend a lot of time watching *Jeopardy*, if my mother is any example.)

Anyway, it's 7:15. They might as well come home and start their baths. I push open the holey, stretched-out screen door, step out into the muggy Texas evening, and hear them, shouting in the empty lot two doors down. Doubtless they are over there playing ball with Daniel Dominguez's father.

Thank God for Daniel Dominguez's father, who

has extra fathering energy to spread around—not just to my kids, but to the teenage sons of a single mom down the street. He roughhouses, goes fishing, plays soccer, rides bikes, throws baseballs, and even takes this ragtag bunch to exotic locales such as the one Vincie described as "one of those Chinese places with pool tables." The Chinese pool hall turned out to be Pato's Tacos, but you can see how occasionally, even in our politically correct era, the distinction between the cuisines of various peoples with shiny black hair can be a little confusing.

I walk across the fresh-cut, verdant yard of the next-door-neighbors Lori Ann and Clyde, a couple notable for their wholesome good looks and horrifying industry. As usual, they are out in their driveway washing their red Isuzu Trooper with huge buckets of soapy water, sponges, hoses and rags. "How come we never wash our car, Mom?" Hayes asked me recently.

"Some people have clean cars, dear, and others have children," I told him.

The empty lot between Lori Ann and Clyde's and the Dominguezes' is the local ballfield, driving range and playground, and it is there that I find the boys and Dan kicking a soccer ball around.

"Come on, boys," I call. "It's time for your bath."

For once, they don't immediately burst into wails of protest; they must be tired. Vince trudges obediently toward me, his cheeks smudged with sweat and dirt, his scratched-up knees peeping out beneath the edge of his humongous T-shirt. Hayes—well, actually Hayes isn't coming; he's running to get the ball and dribble it down the field one more time.

When I was a kid, my father used to say that most child behavior could be explained by his One More Bounce theory—that a kid always has to do whatever he's being told to stop doing just one more time, so that he or she can have the illusion of making the decision him- or herself. I'm not stopping because *you* said so, the child wants you to know, but because I feel like it.

I beckon; he runs. I call; he punts. I think my father would have to modify his theory for Hayes. With him, it's a minimum of three more bounces. "Okay, Hayes Anthony Winik, you come right now or you'll wake up tomorrow morning in military school!"

He passes the ball to Dan, calls goodbye, and trots wearily toward us.

"I was *coming*, Mom," he pants.

"In your own special way," I reply, taking his hot little hand in one of mine, and Vincie's in the other, and the three of us swing our arms walking back to the house.

◎ ◎ ◎

"Okay!" I shout, turning off the faucets. "Bath is ready! Clothes in the laundry, bodies in the tub!"

"But Mom, it's not even night," Vincie complains as he slides into the bubbles. He hasn't gotten used to daylight savings time yet, and he's too little to recall the rhythm of lengthening days from years past. "Why do we have to go to bed in the middle of the day when everyone else in the whole world is still out playing!"

I try to explain it to him as I wipe his face with a blue washcloth, seeing how much dirt I can get off before he remembers he doesn't need my help.

"Mom!" Hayes calls from my room.

I go in and find my nine-year-old stretched out mostly naked on the bed, tossing discarded clothes across the room into the hamper from a supine position.

"He shoots!—He scores!—Three points!" His shockingly big feet are suddenly in my face. "Could you help me get these shoes and socks off, please Mom? It's really hard to get them off when you're all sweaty."

I pull off the ole cowboy's boots and spurs and he ambles down the hall to join his brother in the bubble bath.

"Use soap!" I call. "Wash your hair!"

"Can we watch cartoons after bath?"

"Not if you want to have story." I pick up the clothes that didn't make the three-point hamper shot, pair up the scattered sneakers as a first line of defense against tomorrow's inevitable cries of Where are my shoes?, then go down the hall and poke my head in the bathroom to see what's going on. Oh no.

"How can there be two inches of water on the floor already? You just got in here!"

"Hayes spilled," Vincie explains.

"I was just trying to get a drink," Hayes says, looking down sheepishly.

Well, that explains the giant plastic cup lying in the middle of our new pond.

"Why not use the faucet in the bathtub instead of trying to reach all the way to the sink, Hayes?" I sigh as I bend down to clean up.

"He did it on accident, Mom," Vince tells me, in a rare moment of fraternal solidarity.

"I know, sweetie. I'm just getting tired." I tell myself what a great and wonderful parent I am for remaining so calm in the face of this latest threat to sanity. (You have to give yourself credit for the little things—there may not be anything else.) I continue in my best Mother of the Year voice: "How 'bout if you guys finish up washing your hair and brushing your teeth without any more accidents and without me having to ask fifteen times?"

I shuffle down to their room, an eleven-by-ten-foot furniture warehouse containing L-shaped bunk beds, two dressers, two desks, two bookshelves, all artfully stacked and layered so you can just about thread your way among them, to lay out their night shirts. Tonight it's Austin Hot Sauce Festival for Hayes and AIDS Walk for Life for Vince. I locate the current bedtime book, turn off the overhead light, and turn on the reading lamp and night light.

This must be my lucky day—I hear the water draining out of the bath *and* the electric toothbrushes. "Floss?" I yell hopefully, laying my suddenly weary bones down on the floor on the Dallas Cowboys area rug. In a moment, I hear stomping and grunting in the hall, and catch a glimpse as they parade by, stark naked, actually flossing their teeth and doing some kind of tribal dance.

Oral hygiene among the bushmen, oogah oogah ooh.

"Mommy," says Vince a few minutes later, all clean and flossed and tucked in his bed. "How come I can't lose a tooth?"

"You can, honey. You just haven't yet."

"Is it true that the tooth fairy is really Daniel's mother?"

"What?"

"Daniel got two dollars when his tooth fell out and he said really his mother put it there."

"Oh, I see."

"So is she? Is Tomi the tooth fairy?"

"No, honey, as far as I know she's a social worker."

Hayes peeks down from the upper bunk. "But—"

I give him a cautionary look and interrupt to prevent further bean-spilling. "Hayes. Do you want me to continue with *Little Men* or should I read that book you brought home from the school library?"

"What about *my* book from the school library?" Vincie interjects, yawning.

"We'll just have *Little Men*," I say, to forestall an argument. I start reading a chapter titled "John Brooke," and find, to my consternation, that it is about the sudden death of Meg's husband, young Demi and Daisy's father. Another dead daddy! I still haven't gotten over the shock of taking my kids to the *The Lion King* not long after Tony died, and discovering that not only is the father lion killed, but it's indirectly the son's fault, then when things get really tough, Dad sends a helpful message from beyond the grave. Give me a break, please. However, the boys were fine; I think it makes them feel less alone to hear about children dealing with the loss of a parent, even if there are unrealistic elements or if, as in stories like

The Little Princess, it turns out the father isn't really dead after all. Surely we can count on Louisa May for strong characters, sound advice, and keeping the dead dead once they have died. I plunge ahead.

The chapter seems to go on forever, with the news of the death, the reactions, the funeral, more reactions, then finally Demi's return to school after a few weeks. " 'He seldom spoke of his loss,' " I read, " 'but Aunt Jo often heard a stifled sobbing in the little bed at night; and when she went to comfort him, all his cry was, "I want my father! Oh, I want my father!"— for the tie between the two had been a very tender one, and the child's heart bled when it was broken.' "

Vincie stops me right there. "He shouldn't think about it all the time," he says exasperatedly. "Of course he feels sad if he thinks about his dad every minute. He should like go out and play with his friends and go to school and think about other stuff."

Out of the mouths of babes, as they say. "Well, Vince," I say, shaking my head, "that's good advice, but in the story it's only a couple weeks since his father died, so of course he's still very upset. In the beginning it's hard to think of other stuff. Remember? Remember how sad we were at first?"

"A couple weeks? I thought it was like two years or something."

"No, sweetie, it just happened. He just came back to school."

"Well, gah, it seemed like a hundred and million hours. This book is too long!"

"Maybe we've had enough for one night, then."

"No!" This cry of dissent comes from the upper bunk.

"I thought you were sleeping, Raisin."

"No, Mama. Can't you please finish the chapter?"

"It's not making you sad?"

"No," he asserts, but I hear something else in his voice. "Mom, how old is Demi?"

"He's about your age, I think, about nine."

He takes that in for a minute. "But I was only six when my dad died."

"Right."

"I don't understand how did his dad get the fever."

"It doesn't really say, Hayes. But in those days people got sick and died easier than today."

"Okay, just read."

A soft snore from the nearby pillow indicates that our bereavement counselor has checked out for the evening.

"I'll read you a couple more pages, but then I have to stop so Vincie doesn't miss too much."

Soon I am too tired to go on. Hoping Hayes is asleep, I flick out the light.

"Mom!" He is already padding down the ladder.

"What are you doing?"

"I have to make a peepee and give you a kiss."

I wait for him to come back from the bathroom, which he does momentarily, rubbing his eyes, then stretching his arms around me for a hug.

"Okay, baby, it's late now. Climb up there and sleep fast."

"Goodnight, Mama." He turns to go up the ladder.

"Goodnight, my sweet little boy."

8

Housework

I work at home in a small, sunny room with fuchsia windowsills, plank-and-cinderblock bookshelves, and an immense tabby cat draped over the fax machine, stamping muddy paw prints on all incoming documents. Between working here, living here and serving in the capacities of head custodian, kitchen manager, human services coordinator and night nurse, it's safe to say I don't get out of the house much. I spend so much time in this house, I sometimes think of the building itself as a kind of super-body, its walls a second skin, myself a cell circulating through it, pumped from the auricle kitchen to the ventricle couch.

As remote as it seems now, there was a time when I "worked outside the home," as it is put of late, with tacit lip service to women's domestic labors. Yes, once upon a time in a far-off condominium, when I first started my project of having children, I had a real job. I was a technical writer for a software company. I had

125

worked there full-time for five years when Hayes was born. It was a small start-up with a lot of work to do, and many of us became happy workaholics doing it. We were young, we were childless: that company was our baby. We worked nights, Saturdays, holidays, whatever it took.

However, when Hayes arrived in the spring of '88—a truly long-awaited event, as I had had the nightmare of a full-term stillborn baby the year before, gotten pregnant with Hayes a month after that, and had thus been "expecting" for almost two years— I was sure I would want to stay at home with him for a while. I arranged a three-month maternity leave and bid my coworkers adieu when I went into labor. Finally, I would have my baby, and I planned to devote every scrap of time and energy to his nurture.

However, as soon as the initial glow wore off, I wasn't sure I was right for the job. Fading into the distance behind me was my familiar adult life—my job, my business trips, my lunch dates, my circle of childless friends. Ahead, the weeks seemed to stretch like a desert, with only a few hundred diaper changes as landmarks. Without the schedules of the workplace, daily traffic with grown-ups, without completable projects and predictable paychecks, I felt adrift. Hayes was cute, but he wasn't much of a conversationalist.

Suddenly, I was spending whole days in a neighborhood I had never seen except after dark or on weekends. Instant aficionado of nearby parks and sidewalks, I wondered wistfully who lived behind all those closed doors. I found myself dawdling in front of houses which showed signs of baby life—a stroller on the porch, a baby swing glimpsed through a window—thinking something like "Won't you please come out and play?"

It wasn't the baby that was causing the trouble. He was almost too easy. No, the problem child was me. Here I was, supposed to be having the Most Fulfilling Experience of My Life, but somehow it didn't feel like my life at all. My body had made the leap from pregnancy to maternity, but my personality (at least the part that conducted conversations with other adults) had been left behind. I was disoriented, lonely, even, God forgive me, bored.

Hayes was probably not much more than a week old when I called in and had the shipping clerk schlep my computer and several boxes of work-in-progress over to my apartment. Not long after, I showed up back in the office, babe in arms. I couldn't stay away. I needed to work. I needed to talk, to schmooze. I needed all kinds of activity and interaction mothering a newborn didn't provide. But he was entirely too tiny to be put in day care, we couldn't afford a nanny, and in any case, I couldn't stand the thought of letting someone else take care of him. I didn't want to be separated from him at all. However, he proved entirely too adorable to have around the office. Furthermore, my breast-feeding at business meetings in the conference room with toys spread out all over the floor on a baby blanket was not as warmly received by management as I had hoped, nor was the cooptation of the receptionist as mother's helper.

I was able to work out a virtually idyllic solution: I went part-time, working until mid-afternoon, and Tony went to the salon where he cut hair when I got home. We were really lucky; this arrangement lasted for several years, through our move out of the condo and into a real house with a yard, through the birth of our second child, the one-time Baby Messiah.

By the time I quit my job in 1994, "idyllic" was not a word one would have applied to life among the Winiks. We had one kid in kindergarten and another in a half-day preschool program. Their father was very sick with AIDS and was falling apart emotionally as well; work for him was a thing of the past and even driving a car was becoming a dubious project. Meanwhile, my first book had just been published, and I was starting to have opportunities to earn money writing and speaking. So many things were demanding my attention, I was about to lose my mind. It was a miracle if I could even find time to show up at the office.

Something had to go. The job may not have looked like the most expendable thing, but there really was no alternative except to abandon my writing. I couldn't do that, not after two decades of trying to get where I had finally arrived. I figured if it didn't work out financially, I'd just crawl back to the software company on my hands and knees.

By this time, I hated my job anyway. Our start-up had been bought by a company from California with a much more centralized, traditional corporate culture, and most of my old friends (including the original owners) were long gone. The office had come to seem a drab, fluorescent-lit prison, and writing manuals and datasheets and advertisements held no more interest for me than breaking rocks. It was time to make a run for it.

When I finally gathered the nerve to leave my job (my health insurance, my vacation pay, my postage meter), I pictured myself embarking on a life of freedom, creativity, and meaningful work. At last, I would be a Real Writer. I could picture myself at my desk in my little home office, a ray of sunlight working its way across the hardwood floor as I churned away at my computer, the clicking of the keys the only sound, the arrival of the postman the only interruption. My children? Off playing happily in progressive classrooms filled with art supplies and Lego blocks, leaving me hours of unbroken concentration. Peace and quiet. Total solitude.

Total solitude?

The very thought of it struck terror into my heart.

Sitting here three years later, in my silent house in my deserted neighborhood, I suppose I'm on slightly better terms with solitude than I used to be. But only slightly. I still have most of the same feelings that plagued me during maternity leave. I miss having a job. I miss people. Sometimes I even miss getting dressed in the morning. When you work at an office, or a store, or a plant—any "place of business"—you feel like a part of society if you simply put on your shoes and show up. Maybe not a vital part, but at least somehow connected. You can do nothing for quite a while without even noticing it, or certainly without it bothering you in the least. When you do nothing at home, it's totally different. Two days of nothing and I feel like some boring, overprivileged, suburban slug, some manic-depressive in the depressive state. I'm killing time, and time's killing me back. Maybe the office was a prison, but at least it wasn't solitary confinement.

These days, my only companion is a big fat fly who just came in the back door, and I look back on those days at the office as a nonstop party. There were meetings and collaborations, coffeepot rendezvous, closed-door confessions. Home renovation plans and sex acts were diagrammed on the washable white boards; birthday celebrations and happy hours were plotted on the marketing calendar; split-ups and other tough breaks were felt by us all. Some days, the e-mail system seemed to function mainly as a high-tech note-passing device, messages flying back and forth like scraps of paper in a high school study hall.

Everything happened at that office. Like I said, I even went into labor there, and the vice president of sales drove me home.

As I learned immediately upon beginning my voluntary exile, isolation is only part of the home worker's problem. By way of illustration, I offer this entry from my journal, written on my first day working at home three years ago:

Today is the first day of the rest of my life and I'm in trouble. Got up at six-thirty, fed and dressed kids, made their lunches. Once they were gone, paid bills and balanced checkbook. Read every word of newspaper, returned phone calls, tweezed eyebrows, rolled up extension cords in laundry room. Dyed hair red. Drank far too much coffee, wandered in and out of house, tried without success not to stuff face and smoke cigarettes continuously. Now it is 1:45. Ready for a drink. Only one more hour til I pick up the kids, thank God.

I had discovered the second major peril of working at home. Aside from mind-numbing loneliness, we self-employed, home-based, and telecommuting workers must daily face the mesmerizing vortex of The House itself. The refrigerator, the coffeepot, the bathroom, the television, and the endless cycle of domestic chores, which are no sooner finished than they have to be done again. The tubes of toothpaste with the tops off. The puddles of pee under the toilet. The unread newspapers, the sticky counters, the crusty brownie pan. Soon I began to wonder how I managed at all when I worked in the office, since I found I could easily make a day of folding the laundry and emptying the dishwasher. Half the time, I prefer it that way. Sweeping the kitchen is really so much more satisfying and doable than any of the half-baked projects I've got going on my PowerBook and its electronic brethren.

I may not have any colleagues, but I at least have my business machines to keep me company. My warm relationship with office equipment goes back to my aqua and white Smith Corona electric typewriter, given to me as a present when I went off to college, for years my most treasured possession. Its obnoxious humming was the sound of my thoughts. Its filled-in *g*, muddy *x* and slightly-above-the baseline capital *R* were my handwriting. Its swingy jam back to the margin when I pressed Return—*rrrrrrm, bing!*— made each line typed a public event. When it was on, I was on. We vibrated as one. Me and that Smith Corona: we were poets together, communards, we were Marxist feminist hitchhikers. We stayed up all night and wrote love letters that would break your heart.

As it aged, the typewriter began to show signs of wear. The hesitant *j* key could no longer find its way home in the fan of letters and left an inky kiss on my fingers when I untangled it from the *h* and the *k*. Its oscillations grew too powerful for its plastic frame. Trembling and whining beneath my fingers, it would gradually scoot toward me across the desk until I had to push it away like an overaffectionate pet. *Stay, baby, you stay.*

Hayes, asked years ago what his mother did for a living, told someone I was a typewriter. What does he tell them now? That I'm a laser printer? I hope not. It's a cooler, more mature relationship I have with my electronic devices: my svelte gray laptop, my fax/copier, my phone lines and modems, my e-mail address. All of these I acquired during my first year at home because, of course, I needed them for work. That was not untrue, but their more frequent use is as a means of distracting myself, of re-creating that social buzz I missed so much. I was trying to work, honest, but the phone rang, someone beeped in on call waiting, an e-mail message came, and look, I got a fax! And if no one calls, if there are no incoming faxes, no e-mail, no messages on my tape, I narrow my eyes and stare at my dormant machines, willing them to action. Come on, guys. Get with it.

If worse comes to worst, I take the initiative. I call my sister at her office, or my mother, or some other poor home-based worker and make sure they're not getting anything done either. How about lunch? How about a matinée? What did you do this weekend? Most of the time, these home-working friends are amenable to distraction. After forty-five minutes, we decide what we really need is some exercise. We meet in the park for a vigorous walk. And who, may I ask, are all those other grown-ups on the hike-and-bike trail at 11 A.M.?

It's gotten to the point that when I really must do something, like finish writing something on deadline, I have to leave my house. I take my computer to a coffee shop where I know there will be no interruptions. They even make the coffee for you. I make myself stay there until I've accomplished something (or until the battery in the laptop runs out) because I know once I get home, it's telecommunications time again. This worked fine until one day the guy behind the counter at the coffee shop came up and tapped me on the shoulder. There's a call for you, he said.

Ideally, I suppose, the house should have a split personality. From 7:45 to 2:45, it should be all business. There should be no planning of dinner parties, killing of cockroaches, tweezing of eyebrows, fixing of toilets. I should stay in my office, I should do my work. I should not jump up in the middle of a sentence to look for the lost soccer shin guards or to empty the coffee filter. I should not detour on the way back from the bathroom to put away stray sneakers and jacks, or to figure out what's making that weird smell in the refrigerator. All that can wait until after the kids come home. *Then* I should take off my thinking cap and put on my apron. I should start the dinner, supervise homework, put in a load of towels.

But unfortunately, the boundaries are more fluid than that. My responsibilities as a mother, a wage earner, and a homemaker won't sort themselves out according to schedule. In the morning, when I should be working, I am plagued by the grocery list and the unmade beds. In the afternoon, when "work" is "over," all the zeal of housewifery escapes me. I sneak wistful looks at the computer, suddenly filled with ideas and obsessed by work left unfinished. The phone, obstinately silent all morning, starts to ring with important business calls, and I end up with the portable tucked under my ear, talking to a fact checker in a clean cubicle in a tall skyscraper in a far-off city, doubtless wearing panty hose, while I am battering pork chops, breaking up a sharing war, and enforcing television rules.

"What was your source on this divorce statistic?" she asks, as egg splashes onto my glasses.

"Divorce statistic? Oh, right. Wait a minute. No, Hayes!! Don't maul your brother. Stop! Let's see, I think I got it from the 1970 census—excuse me. Vincie, that's the fakest crying I've ever heard! You're in time out, both of you!"

"I'm really sorry to call you at home," she says in a tone of polite frustration.

I have to laugh. Where else?

9

Sex and Drugs and Good Advice

"Where's Hayes?" I yell out the back door when the half-hourly head count yields one less kid than I expect—and the visible ones are giggling and staring up at the roof.

"He's on the roof," Vincie confirms.

"On the roof?? You're kidding me! He's not allowed on the roof! What in God's name is he doing up there?"

"It's okay, Mom. He's just getting Daniel's Nerf dart."

Well then. No problem. Just getting the Nerf dart. "Tell him to come down right this minute!"

"He is, Mom. He's coming now."

When I fly out there to find out exactly how he plans to get down, I see a wobbly tower of ice chests stacked upon a yellow plastic kiddie picnic table. Vincie and Daniel are holding the edifice steady while

Hayes lowers himself from the carport, his toe carefully locating the lid of the uppermost cooler. He presents Daniel with the Nerf dart and gives me a crooked grin.

"Don't worry, Mom. I do it all the time."

"You do??"

"I'm careful! I swear!"

He *is* careful, it's true. Much more careful than I ever was. When I was exactly his age, nine years old, I got up on the roof of my parents' ranch-style suburban home—and took a flying leap from its eaves. There was no Nerf dart involved, either, no reasonable enterprise or kindly mission. No, it was just a dare. I could not say no to a dare, or anything that looked like one; I had the idea that I was—or should at least try to be—immune to fear. So I balanced on the storm gutter, clutched the window frame behind me, and repeated my mantra: *I am not afraid of anything.* To prove it, I had to turn off the reasonable part of my brain and proceed on automatic pilot.

I did not learn from this experience. Or at least I did not learn the right thing. Not the terrifying fall to earth, not the crash landing in the rose garden, not the sprained fingers or the horrified parents or the two weeks without *Gilligan's Island*—none of these made the primary lasting impression. They were all overruled by the fact that I had done it, I had survived it, I had made it in one piece. The impulsive, reckless, fearless Marion Winik lived to brave new risks and accept new dares, to reject all sound advice, to explore any self-destructive impulse.

And she did. And kept learning that she was invincible, until she learned that she wasn't.

Because for most of my life I have refused to learn any but the hard way, I have done a great many stupid things at least once. I am finished now. I will never again jump off a roof, or swim in the northern Atlantic Ocean in the middle of winter. I will never sneak around to all the other girls' rooms in the dorm at sleepaway camp and steal their little china animals. I no longer shoplift tubes of mascara from Sears or hitchhike to the boardwalk or to California. No one could convince me that spraying Right Guard into a bath towel and sniffing it is a great idea, and not many of the mind-altering experiences I had after that bear repeating, either. I can no longer imagine sleeping by the side of an interstate highway or under a bridge, having sex with a stranger, or dyeing my hair purple or blue.

As an older teenager and a young adult, I looked for positive role models: examples of creative women, women of achievement, power and drama. I found

Sylvia Plath, who died, and Anne Sexton, who died, and Zelda Fitzgerald and Amelia Earhart, who died. There was Janis Joplin, who died, and Frida Kahlo, who died as well. To be a nonconforming woman of inner depth seemed to be a direct route to the funeral home, and I spent much of my twenties tracing that dark path. Excess, self-abuse and violent despair seemed to be essential characteristics of the female artist, and I did my best to excel. Only once again, I was lucky enough to live through it.

When I decided to become a mother, things had to change. The part of me that never stops wanting to do crazy things became my enemy, not my hero. I have to fight it whenever it rears its head; I have stayed up nights wondering to what extent it lives in my children. After all, I grew up idolizing my father, a rule-breaking individualist with a wild streak that zigzagged through all his stories of his childhood, his school years, even his Marine career. I'm sure I somehow perceived my most dangerous, willful decisions, ones that caused him no end of worry, as following in his footsteps. But he was climbing out the window of the science classroom; I was smoking hash. Trying to extend that analogy to Hayes and Vince makes me feel ill.

Hayes, as I said, is a relatively cautious child. He doesn't like to get far away from me in a crowd, or wander off in a field in the dark. He hates the really crazy rides at carnivals and amusement parks, and in any crowd scene acts the role of mother hen, anxiously keeping track of the other kids. When he gets off a roof, he steps onto a cooler. I hope this lasts. Vince, on the other hand, already shows telltale signs of the family inclination. He is always covered with scabs and bruises and never knows where they came from. He rollerblades and bike-rides like a nut and likes to see how long he can keep his head under water. When he says he's running away from home, he actually goes out the door.

If he is as determined to test the limits as I was—as his father was, too—I'm afraid nothing will stop him. Can it be different somehow? Have times changed at all? Can I teach him anything?

About a year ago, a friend and I were at a fast-food restaurant having coffee and watching the kids on the playscape when four police cars screeched into the parking lot. Within minutes, the teenagers who'd been laughing in a corner had been escorted off and driven away.

My friend's four-year-old asked, "Why did the policemen take them?"

"Drugs," said Vincie, nodding sagely. "It must have been drugs."

"What's drugs?" replied the little one.

"Well—I don't know," said my son, "But it's really, really bad. Right, Mom?"

Uh-oh, I was thinking, do we have to talk about this already? I thought I had a few more years to figure it out. But no. Already they have assemblies at school to warn them about drugs, alcohol and cigarettes. Anyone who lights up in our house gets a lecture from the kids about smoking, and if they don't care enough about their own lungs, we move on to the dangers of passive smoke. "That could get in my lungs and kill me," Vincie will tell you, and you better not get caught chucking recyclable items in the garbage can, either, or filling up the bathtub more than six inches deep.

"You know, Mommy," Vincie said, as I pulled the cork from a bottle of Argentine red, "if you drink too much beer you go insane."

"I know, Vincie. I know all about it."

This brainwashing isn't all bad, no sir. Thanks to it, I am among the many parents who have either quit smoking, or at least quit smoking in front of their kids. But there are some parts of the message that concern me. Does the party line have room for this mommy's checkered past? I mean, when they hear just how much "beer" I've drunk in my day, how will it make sense that I'm not insane?

Yes, boys, I may be your homeowning, Jeep-driving, Cub Scouts-and-soccer mom now, but my past includes a major walk on the wild side. I tried every drug known to man, and at twenty-six married a gay ice skater who shared my bad habits—that is, your father. Though I managed to clean up my act before you were born, your dad struggled with a drug problem until he died. And I couldn't hide all this from you even if I wanted to, for I've written and spoken about it. My past is in print and in public.

Though I may represent an extreme, I'm certainly not the only parent at the plant sale with a history. People my age grew up in a radically different era, during the Great American Love-In and Pot Party, when experimenting with drugs and sex was both philosophically ennobled and almost routine. Late-vintage boomers like me may have had it the worst— more debauchery, less idealism by the time the seventies came along. Ours was a different time in many ways. Back then, you didn't die from making love, and some of the scariest drugs were barely invented. I wasn't the only person who really believed that this abandoned lifestyle was just part of being young—even part of some better world we were trying to imagine—not just a criminal grab bag of self-destructive, venal, antisocial behaviors.

That was my time, this is yours. Now the culture says drugs are bad—"really, really bad," right,

Vince?—and most of us former hippies would have to agree. I, for one, am completely clear on the fact that I don't want drugs to affect your lives the way they did mine. I spent a lot of my school years loaded, or coming down. I had friends who died driving drunk, others who got sent to reform school, others who ended up in jail or mental institutions. And while I admit to having had at least a little fun in the bad old days, there was always a dark side. There were broken hearts and unwanted pregnancies and out-of-control situations. There were funerals. Virtually all of the people closest to me ended up with drug problems that reverberated far into their adult lives. Those of us who lived through it are stuck with "issues," hopefully dormant, forever.

Put it this way: I may joke about the brain cells I've killed, but God knows I wish I still had them.

Whatever combination of inner strength and luck got me through college and graduate school and landed me two decades later with a decent life and two beautiful sons, I know I can't count on your having inherited it. Your father, two uncles and many others who would have loved you so much aren't here to watch you grow up. They are dead now from the lifestyle we all shared.

While I would like it if you didn't do drugs at all, if and when you do—one estimate says 95 percent of high school kids try either drugs or alcohol before they graduate—maybe you'll let me share a little expertise. Who knows more about this than me? Maybe if I don't paint everything black-and-white, we can discuss the shades of gray. I'd like to help you distinguish between life-threatening risks—getting in a car with a drunk driver, unsafe sex, mixing tranquilizers and alcohol—and questionable choices. I could talk about the value of waiting—the older and more mature you are when you experiment, the more likely you can handle the result. Let's talk about the difference between heroin and marijuana, between selling drugs and doing them. I think my best hope of having an influence on your lives comes from not being in denial, from keeping the lines of communication open. Doesn't this begin with telling the truth about myself?

Which is harder than it sounds. To tell your story you've got to figure out what your story is and how it relates to your current values—a process even I, who do it nine to five, am still working on. What I've figured out so far is that I am not the perfect factory-issue role model. I still have some ambivalence, some adolescent defiance. Talking about my "past," as if it were a neatly wrapped package taped up and gathering dust in the attic for years, doesn't ring true. This box is not even shut yet. Anyone who uses even alcohol—to me, different from some of the illegal drugs only in its legality—is in the same situation. As your aunt Nancy says, "It's not about them learning from your mistakes. It's about you learning from them."

Even if I am still a work-in-progress, I can at least teach you to cling to the lifeline that's got me this far. Which is telling, or at least trying to tell the truth.

Am I really going to give this speech? Sure. In fact, I just gave it, in a sort of delayed-action way.

I would only temper that "sure" with something I learned about telling the truth to kids during Tony's struggle with AIDS. Which is that you have to tell children things they can understand in amounts they can handle. Otherwise, you're just overwhelming them. My boys are still young and relatively innocent. But because they've lived through so much already, I'm getting a lot of practice in answering tough questions. Since their father died, I have answered the question "How did Daddy get AIDS?" many times. They recently became dissatisfied with a simple "He got it from someone else who had it." When I explained that AIDS is transmitted by sharing drugs or making love with an infected person, my six-year-old offered this deduction: "So Daddy must have had a girlfriend before you who died of AIDS."

"Well," I said, "it could have been a boyfriend."

Vincie made a you-gotta-be-kidding-me face. And while their father's primary sexual orientation has never been a secret, I could see that this was not the time to go into it. My sons have their own truth about their daddy—in their memory, he was a lot like John Travolta in *Look Who's Talking*—dancing, cracking jokes, tough but sweet, head-over-heels for the kids and Mommy too. I hope they never lose that idea, because they are right.

But I also want them to know the rest of the story—how very little fun he had during the years of his life that were controlled by addiction, how unsafe sex he had when he was young killed him before he had the chance to see them grow up. If there is a poster child for Just Say No, Tony was it. So, far from fearing that they'll someday read my books, as some people critically presume, I wrote the books more for them than for anybody else. In the absence of any sure knowledge of the straight and narrow and how to make people hew to it, I want them to have the gift of the truth, and the gift of telling it.

Some things never change.

Recently, Tony's parents came down to visit the boys for a week; I took the opportunity to go to Montreal with Robb (of whom they seemed to guardedly approve.) The second night, I persuaded our Canadian hosts to take us to a nightspot near their home in the Laurentians. The place proved to be an indoor-outdoor Partyworld, with not just pool, pinball and Pac-Man, but the latest in bar sports: bungee jumping. Apparently, after a few drinks, some people will do *anything* to impress their date.

When the owner of the club came over to say hello, he offered Robb a complimentary bungee jump. "It normally costs seventy-five bucks," he said, "but you can try it for free."

"Uh, thanks very much," he said, "but—"

"*I'll* do it," I interrupted, as little equipped to resist a bargain as a challenge. I looked briefly over at the current victim, dangling upside-down on the bungee just a few feet above a pond, his jacket and shirt hanging over his face to expose his pale chest. Without giving anyone a chance to talk me out of it, I walked straight to the registration booth, signed a release without reading it, had my weight written on my hand so the cord length could be adjusted, and set about scaling the sixteen stories of ladders to the platform.

At the top, two young fellows bound my feet and asked if I had any questions. Only one, in response to which they informed me that, so far, no one had died bungee jumping at this location. Did I want to hit the water or not? they asked. I thought not.

Fast losing the ability to hear, see or breathe as a result of the terror I had vowed to ignore, I was escorted to the edge of the platform. Almost immediately, I plunged off the edge. The sensation, insofar as I could have a sensation at that point, was absolute, linear, consciousness-erasing thrill. The cord quickly reached its full extension and began contracting erratically, bouncing me wildly up and down, left and right. I didn't like that part too much. My body was completely limp when two more young fellows showed up in a rubber raft, untied my feet and guided me into the boat.

I know that a single parent—any parent, probably, should not bungee jump. That was stupid. I won't do it again. But the bungee jumper inside me lives, and I want her to help me figure out what to say to Vincie when I see him skateboarding down the driveway into the street.

Yes, skateboard.

Yes, fast and wild.

Yes, with pads and a helmet, and no, not down the driveway into the street.

And then I will have to let him go. And breathe deep, and sit back, and watch.

8:59 P.M.

"Goodnight, Mama."

"Goodnight, my sweet little boy."

Our evening ritual is over; the poignant bedtime scene draws to a close. With a deep breath that is half sigh, half yawn, I depart the bedroom, leaving the door open the prescribed width—the distance from my elbow to my wrist—and arrange the hallway lighting scheme that has so effectively deterred midnight monsters for several years now. I stop in the kitchen to get a cup of chamomile tea and the portable phone on the way toward what will pass for heaven tonight: the living room couch. I sink heavily into its cushions, which still smell like guinea pig pee six months after Sparky's disappearance. Mental note: Call couch cleaning service. Are they the ones I just hung up on at dinner?

Choices: Flip through *New Yorker*. Read real book. Call sister. Call mother. Call boyfriend, who's probably just finished putting his own kids to bed. Is there anyone I know who would want to rent a movie and come over? As if I would even make it through the credits.

9:04 P.M.

Creak of door opening, footsteps in the hall. Another trip to the bathroom? Okay, whatever. Let it go.

9:10 P.M.

Plaintively: "Mom."

Resignedly: "What."

Tremulously: "Mom?"

Testily: "What, Hayes? I already said 'What.' What?"

Piteously: "I can't sleep."

Sternly: "You've been trying for all of eight minutes, Hayes."

Beseechingly: "But, Mom."

Shakily: "Just close your eyes and go to sleep."

Foolishly: "But—"

Finally: "No more buts! Good night!"

9:20 P.M.

The *New Yorker* seems to be over my head this evening. I pick up a collection of Erma Bombeck columns from the sixties and seventies. Still making harried housewives laugh after all these years, that Erma. Tonight I read a piece about how for her first child, she recorded BMs in his baby book and took pictures every four days for the baby album. By her third kid, birth and graduation were on the same roll of film, and the only thing in his baby book was a Congratulations! card from the insurance agent. (And yet just the other day I read headlines in the newspaper announcing the amazing discovery that birth order does affect personality. Isn't it funny how they keep making startling new discoveries of things that everyone has known since the dawn of time?)

Speaking of birth order affecting personality, I've been thinking about the intensity of my reaction to Hayes and Vince's sibling rivalry. I get so upset when I see Hayes teasing Vince or lording it over him or manipulating him. I tend to rush in like a mad crusader, and usually don't even bother to find out how Vincie may have contributed to the problem. I see what I'm doing—I'm reacting as if Hayes represented the aspect of me that was so mean to my little sister, so competitive and grabby and having to have everything and be in charge of everything. By defending Vince, I can stop the injustice; I can symbolically reverse the whole history of younger sibling abuse. But sometimes I think I'm so busy protecting Vince that I overdo it.

Mental note: Be nicer to Hayes.

9:32 P.M.

Hayes, from the bedroom: "Mom, I'm hungry."

"Tough."

"What was for dinner again?"

"Pork chops!"

"Oh, yeah."

"Go to sleep, Hayes."

"Can I just have a glass of water?"

Sigh. "Come out and get it."

Hair mussed, face flushed, he comes blinking into the kitchen.

"Just have a sip or you'll be going to the bathroom fifty more times. And hurry! You're never going to get out of bed tomorrow."

"Okay, Mommy."

He gives me a little wave on his way back to bed.

9:42 P.M.

Flipping through *Parenting* magazine. Ha! An article about putting your kids to bed. I've read plenty of these, I know what they say. You have to be firm. Just let 'em cry and whine and complain. Etc. And if you just sit through it and don't give in, everything will be fine.

This brings to mind the first night I made Hayes

and Vince sleep in their own room instead of in my bed. Though Robb was part of the inspiration for this change, I put it into effect on a night when he wasn't here, so the kids wouldn't blame him for their exile. Good thing, since I would hardly have wanted an audience for the ensuing scene. For a solid hour after I put them to bed, they kept up a constant wailing. To stop myself from giving in, going nuts or running out the front door, I sat at my desk and made myself write down everything they said. It went like this:

"Why does Mommy have to be so mean? Come here, Mommy. I can't handle this, Mommy. I need someone to sleep with me. I can't stand this. Why do you have to make new rules up every day? You're stupid, Mommy. I can't breathe, Mommy. It's really bad. Super, super bad. It hurts really super bad! Mommy, I have to tell you something. Mommy, it's important. Mommy! Can't you hear me, Mommy? Don't you have ears or something, Mommy? I hate it up here. I want to be with Mommy! Owweee! Owwwee! My throat hurts really bad! You don't understand me, Mommy! You don't understand anything!"

I could hardly believe I lived through it. But the next night they went straight to sleep like a miracle. Why is it still somehow annoying when the articles in *Parenting* magazine prove correct?

Tentatively: "Mom?"

Exhaustedly: "Oh, Hayes. It's ten o'clock at night. I'm tired. Your full-service parent is closed for the night."

Desperately: "Please, Mom, can I just have one more kiss?"

I was an insomniac, too, when I was a kid. I would toss and turn for hours until my sheets were hot and tangled, my stuffed animals were all over the floor, and not a single cool spot was left on either side of the pillow. Meanwhile, my sister would be over in her bed, still and peaceful as a rock, and about as much fun. Finally I would jump up and write a note to my parents on my rainbow memo pad telling them that I could not sleep, I would not sleep, it wasn't my fault and why were they torturing me like this? Then I would stomp out to the living room, bang open the louvered doors and throw my note on the floor. They would barely glance up from their card game to say "Go back to bed."

Isn't this a perfect example of one of those things you say as a child you will never forget? You will *never* grow up and do this thing that was done to you to your own kid. You *will* remember what it was like! You will be different.

Quietly: "Please, Mommy."

Oh, Hayes. In I go. I climb up into the top bunk with him, put my head beside his on the pillow, curve my arm around his waist, and pull him toward me. So big, but still my little boy.

Sleepily: "Sing?"

Very softly, I start a James Taylor song I have been singing to him since he was a baby. *There is a young cowboy, he lives on the range . . .* I can feel him relax, breathing regularly now, his body warm and still against mine. The magazines and the phone calls will have to wait, I guess . . .

10

The Birthday Syndrome

It is Sunday morning and there is a huge blue dome tent set up in my living room, the remains of a Troy Aikman piñata smoldering on the barbecue grill, and eight little boys roller skating in and out of my house. (Don't you think somebody could make a fortune with an electronic device for households with children that automatically says "Shut the door, please," every time the door is opened?) I am standing at the stove cooking eggs and sausage for breakfast tacos and counting the minutes until 11 A.M., when this party will be officially over. The parents will drive up and claim their offspring, the piles of skates and sleeping bags and bathing suits will disappear, and the weeklong extravaganza of festivities for Hayes's ninth birthday will come at last to its blessed end. Things have been going pretty well so far, but we're in overtime now, and will not make it to the final buzzer without somebody getting knocked down, somebody locking himself in the guest room with the Game

Boy, and Hayes casting himself on his bed with tears rolling down his face because he is not the central focus of all eyes and ears. "Mom, I don't understand. It's my birthday and nobody's paying any attention to me," he mourns.

Perhaps there is never a birthday that is just right. Perhaps the idea of a major holiday established in one's honor, a day awaited all year long, a day that vies with Christmas in its power to shape the calendar and to galvanize loved ones into a frenzy of preparation, is inevitably doomed to end in overload and/or disappointment. So much waiting! Every few weeks lately, Vincie's been asking, "Mommy, how long till my birthday?"

"It's only August, Vince. You just had your birthday. It's eleven months till the next one."

"How many minutes is that?"

When it finally comes, how can it live up to its hype? Believe me, I try. For example, this recent birthday of Hayes's consisted of all of the following:

On the morning of the Day Itself, there was a pile of presents waiting on the table and a breakfast of chocolate chip pancakes and bacon.

Two dozen cupcakes were sent to school for a party in his third-grade classroom.

Per the young gourmand's request, a dinner of steak, salad, french fries, corn on the cob and a wee glass of champagne was served on the deck by the pool to "the family"—we three, my boyfriend and his girls, and our friends the Shahins, whose son Sam is practically Hayes and Vince's brother.

After that evening's soccer game, during which Hayes kicked the winning goal, a giant homemade Cool Whip cake was served to the assembled Knights and their parents.

The "real" birthday party—all of the preceding was just a warm-up—was scheduled to be an overnight camp-out at a nearby park on Saturday night. When torrential rains made camping impossible, Plan B was quickly devised. Jessica Shahin and I took the eight invitees to a roller-skating rink for a few hours, then to dinner at Spaghetti Warehouse, then home to the Troy Aikman piñata, piles of candy, and a rented copy of *Honey, We Shrunk Ourselves*, after which they curled up in their sleeping bags in the living room until the next morning when they sprang out of their tents at 6 A.M. for S'mores-flavor Pop Tarts, more roller skating, football, baseball and computer golf, cartoons, breakfast tacos, and a second viewing of *Honey, We Shrunk Ourselves*.

So perhaps Hayes's nervous collapse is completely understandable. Who wouldn't throw themselves on the bed in tears after all of this?

Ginny Burnett, a Latin American studies professor and mother of three, comes to pick up her son Willie from the party. We are standing on the porch, watching the kids run back and forth, giving Willie the requested "five more minutes." She says, "Your birthday is right after Hayes's, isn't it?"

"Yep," I say.

"You're not excited?"

"How excited can you get about turning thirty-nine?" I ask her.

"Oh, tell me about it. You know what Willie said to me the other day? He said, 'You've looked exactly the same since I was born, Mom. Your hair is the same, you wear the same clothes, you have the same glasses—only your face keeps getting older and older.'" She laughed ruefully. "I couldn't even get mad at him. It's the truth."

I was a young mother for about ten minutes, I think, one of those energetic girls with cute haircuts and cutoff shorts you see in the park pushing a stroller. Not to say my body didn't show the effects of three consecutive pregnancies—blowing up like the Macy's parade float version of yourself then pop goes the baby then whoosh comes the milk and when it's all over, your feet are a half size bigger, your bra is a cup size smaller, your female parts have been through hell. Fortunately, most of the postpartum impact can be hidden by clothes.

And then, somehow, the damage spreads. One day I looked in the mirror and poof, I was middle-aged. I was no longer a young mom but a regular mom-aged mom, complete with laugh lines, stretch marks and a bottle of covers-only-the-gray L'Oreal hair dye in my shopping cart. Without warning, it had begun: the fading, the wrinkling, the softening.

Recalling vaguely a number of magazine and television ads targeted to women in my situation, I hied to the mall, strode purposefully to the cosmetics counter of a large department store, had a nostalgia attack over the old Clinique skin analysis "computer" with its plastic knobs and sliding panels, and, in this weakened state, paid forty-five bucks for a jar of something with a promising name recommended by a perfect-skinned twenty-two-year-old.

"Simply Amazing Overnight Rejuvenation Treatment," I read. "Sounds terrific."

"My customers love it," she said as I handed her my credit card.

Maybe I just didn't love it enough. Maybe it's like fairy dust—it only works if you truly believe. Maybe not only belief but regular application is required, and it is my haphazard use of the product that's really to blame for its failure to stop the epidermal clock. After three years, I admit, I still haven't used up even half of what's in the jar. The unfortunate truth is I don't have the time to beat back time, not to mention the energy. I doubt I'm the only parent whose evening beauty ritual consists of brushing my teeth. Sometimes, having fallen asleep in the boys' room reading them a story, I wake up only enough to stumble to my bed. I can barely take off my clothes, much less micromanage my complexion with an array of beauty products.

So, you see, I deserve this neck. And in any case, what's the use of looking twenty-five when I feel so very thirty-nine? I am much too tired to be a young mother. Just thinking about staying up late at night and then having to get up to get the kids off to school in the morning exhausts me. An afternoon nap on the other hand, sounds like just the thing. I forget people's names. I forget people's faces. I forget why I walked into the kitchen. I can wring a hangover out of a couple of glasses of red wine. I absentmindedly store my possessions in bizarre places and then have to spend hours searching for them. Where the hell is my wrinkle cream? Who hid my high-potency vitamins?

In fact, my personality is aging even faster than my appearance. The new Old Me comes complete with bourgeois opinions. Although I haven't started watching *Jeopardy* or following the stock market, I am in almost every other way turning into my mother. I have noticed, for example, that it has become a matter of deep personal pride to me to have my children nicely dressed at social functions. I find myself drinking decaf, doing crossword puzzles, and advising friends to marry for money. I can spend hours discussing my own or other people's health problems. After years of brown rice and tofu, I now like a little sardine on rye toast for lunch. After all that hard core partying, big fun is now an occasional cigarette and a gin martini. It's not just my neck and my hands that have begun to look like my mother's—it's my soul. The other day I heard my son call someone a "jerk-off" and her famous line came right out of my mouth.

" 'Jerk' will be sufficient," I briskly informed him.

Oh, yes, they're hearing it all now, all the things I never in a million years imagined I'd say:

"Don't get fresh with me, young man."

"That is not a word we use in this house."

"If Daniel Dominguez told you to run into traffic, would you do that too?"

"Do I look like your slave?"

"Must you wear that *thing?*"

"You just take that mouth of yours and go to your room."

So. Hayes's birthday ends and mine looms. Can't wait! My friend Sue, who turned thirty-nine last year, called to warn me about it. Late at night, when her party was over, she slipped down to the basement alone and started going through boxes of mementos.

She hadn't meant to get maudlin, but there were pictures of her and her ex-husband in their early twenties, programs from long-ago plays and graduations, worn matchbooks, creased letters, faded valentines. She said she felt like a little kid going through her parents' stuff—there was a whole past there, friends and cars, pets and apartments, hairstyles and winter coats that had come and gone. She realized, tears plopping on the torn Grateful Dead tickets, that she's already had a life. That many things are irredeemably over. And she can't even remember the names of half the people in the photographs.

As growing up gives way to growing old, as our bodies fall apart, our idiosyncracies petrify, and our nerves fray by the day if not minute, the yearly celebration of the aging process becomes a little tricky. Yippee! Let's Open the Presents! meets Could Everybody Just Go Away and Leave Me Alone? Even if you still think you want to be the center of the universe, you're probably too cranky to hold up under the attention.

Remember your thirteenth, sixteenth, eighteenth, twenty-first, your twenty-fifth, your thirtieth birthday? With each came a sense of accomplishment, of progress. Looking down from the glorious peak of birthday self-absorption, you could see how far you'd come, how far you still wanted to go.

But then you are there. You are finally—oh, so finally—an adult. Uh-oh. Another birthday. One candle closer to the inferno. And you're supposed to jump up and celebrate your increasing age in a culture that idolizes youth. And those uproarious birthday cards! *Here are some uplifting words for your birthday. Lycra and Spandex.* Ha ha, I say, bent double with laughter. Or is it osteoporosis?

As the concept of birthday as milestone is supplanted by the reality of birthday as millstone, the truth is, we're not talking about birth anymore. The subject is death. In the best of cases, you're more than halfway there, and today you get to hear the ticking very close to your ear. You get black Mylar balloons with your age printed on them. You get a bunch of boxes in the basement that make you cry. You get a lot of cultural shtick built around the serious terror of aging, and maybe a bottle of booze to wash it down.

"What do you want to do on your birthday?" I asked my boyfriend Robb, who is turning forty-five this year, or as he darkly thinks of it, leaving the jejune early forties and entering the hopelessly over-the-hill late forties. Next stop? Well, of course: Fifty.

"Nothing," he told me morosely. "I don't like my birthday. I'd rather not have a birthday."

Doesn't he at least want a Troy Aikman piñata to smack around? Or a nice steak dinner? Does everybody have to end up crying on their birthday?

In truth, birthdays have not been the same for us since our friend Phil's birthday two years ago. Phil, who was Robb's best friend for twenty years. On the May morning of his thirty-ninth birthday, he got up, fed his dog, laid out his best suit, and wrote a quick note. He called the police to tell them what he was going to do so they'd be the first to arrive when it was over. Then he went out into his backyard and shot himself with a gun he'd bought a week before.

I had been trying to pin him down for weeks on how he wanted to spend his birthday, which was just a few days before mine.

"Yeah, maybe we'll do something together," he said. "You go ahead with your plans, okay? I'm just not sure where I'll be."

Suddenly all the vagueness made terrible sense. But Phil? He was our favorite person. So charming, so intelligent, so much fun to be with, so self-effacing, so kind to his friends. He was unbelievably well-read, knew dozens of jokes, was a connoisseur of everything fine. He had nice clothes and a nice house and a pretty blond girlfriend and a new job managing a cool restaurant and we all loved him so much.

So why?

As a person prone to snap decisions, and as one whose dark moments can be pretty damn dark, I sometimes catch myself thinking about—I hate to even type the word—suicide. No, I will never do it. I will never get close. I have the best form of suicide prevention available: two children, who depend completely on me. There is no one else. How could I ever leave them?

The thing about being a mother is that you can't give up. No matter how bad you think you are, even if you've convinced yourself that your children would be better off without you, you are wrong. You have to find a way to be happier, or healthier, or whatever it takes to keep being there for your kids. And even if you can't manage anything but miserable and sick, you still can't leave.

The story goes that before Sylvia Plath stuck her head in the gas oven in that cold English dawn, she put out mugs of milk and plates of toast for her two children. What a chilling detail that is. One last mug of milk and plate of toast—here you go, honey. Were they supposed to sit at the table and have breakfast

while she lay dead on the floor, while the men in uniform came to take her body away?

I know it was a helpless gesture—trying to be a
good mother at the very moment she abandoned her
children forever. As if that one last breakfast could say
I love you.

But it can't. Our friend Phil's mother knew that,
at least: the day she went away forever, she did not
leave a TV dinner on the table for her seven-year-old
son. Only her body, lying on the living room floor
with a gun next to it. Three decades later, on his
thirty-ninth birthday, with a hole in his heart that
would never go away, that no love, no friend, no experience could ever fill or close, in so much pain that he
had worked so hard to keep to himself, he followed
her example. On his birthday—the anniversary of the
first separation, the day both mother and child are
born.

I will never know exactly what was going through
his head before he put the gun to it. I will never stop
wondering why he didn't let us at least try to help.
And I will never stop hearing him tell us that he was
going to be like Jack Benny—thirty-nine forever. Just
like Phil to go out with one last joke.

When I feel darkest, I don't let myself think of
him. I think of his mother, and of Sylvia Plath. I
think of them to make myself mad, to shock myself

out of whatever dark miasma gets me so out of whack. Love has to be tougher than that. It has to be there to put out the mug of milk every day. Once you have children, you've made your choice. You have to live.

The morning I turned thirty-nine, I opened my eyes at 6:15 to find Hayes and Vince whispering beside my bed. "Happy birthday, Mom!" they shouted, ceremoniously presenting me with a cup of coffee. Then they led me to the kitchen, where a big box wrapped in Little Mermaid birthday paper lay on the kitchen table. "Open it, Mommy," urged Hayes.

"Do you want me to help you?" Vincie asked.

"She can do it herself, Vince," Hayes shushed him.

"Why don't both of you help?" I suggested.

We tore off the paper in concert—"Wow! Look at this!" I cried with genuine glee. With surreptitious long-distance fund-raising calls to their grandparents and the cooperation of Robb as shopping chauffeur, the boys had gotten me a pair of Rollerblades. As thrilled as I was, they were even more so, still new to the joys of planning a surprise for someone you love.

After I dropped them at school, I went in to work. But since it was my birthday and I'm such a nice boss, I decided to give everyone the day off. I shut down the computer, disconnected the modem, turned on the answering machine, and sent myself out for the day. I went for a long walk with my friend Jim. I got a great haircut from my friend Lexanne. I had lunch at my favorite Mexican restaurant with two old pals from the computer software company. After school, I went skating with the boys until I fell down and skinned my knees. Then my boyfriend gave me an amethyst necklace and an Italian cream cake.

The highlight of the day arrived unexpectedly, at Vincie's soccer game, when all the Terminators got together at halftime and serenaded me. Ten sweaty little faces, in crimson team shirts and cleats on the green Saint Augustine grass, singing "Happy birthday, dear Vince's Mommy" in their six- and seven-year-old voices.

If it wasn't the center of the universe, it was close enough.

11

Medical Matters

I know a mom who is rumored to have taken her son to the emergency room twelve times before he reached one year of age—and all were false alarms. I suppose I'm at the opposite extreme. If you see me heading to the hospital, I'm probably carrying the body part that has to be reattached in a plastic bag in my purse.

My kids are troupers, but they really don't have much choice. Wimpiness gets you nowhere around here. I am the sort of parent who does not react to any but the most authentic screams, the most panic-stricken shrieks. I say, Show me the bones and the blood. Otherwise, be brave, stop crying, and you know where the Band-Aids are. (This self-help approach results in the use of somewhat appalling numbers of Band-Aids.)

Keep a kid home from school for a case of sniffles or a tummyache? Forget it. I have a proud Winik tradition to uphold here. According to my mother, only "malingerers" missed school for anything that didn't involve projectile vomiting or quarantine mandated by a physician. "What? A stomachache? You want to stay home from school because you have a *stomachache?*" You may as well have suggested staying home for a hangnail. A hangnail, in fact, was often held up as an example of the sort of thing people in families less hale and hearty than ours might take to their beds over.

"I'm not raising a bunch of malingerers here," my mother would mutter blackly, as if failing grades, detention, and juvenile hall might be just around the corner for the sufferer of the alleged stomachache. I didn't help matters the morning in fourth grade I turned up with a hangdog look and a temperature of 106, a number I had produced by gargling with hot water from the tap seconds before. I couldn't believe it—how did she *know?* This escapade secured my reputation in the Malingerer Hall of Fame. I don't think I was ever allowed to stay home from school again for any reason whatsoever.

No, at our house, you combed your sweaty hair across your pale forehead, you chugged back a few speckled pink Coricidin or orange St. Joseph's, and you limped to the bus stop.

Because of their experience with their father's death, Hayes and Vince have an unusual perspective on illness. While most kids seem to enjoy sickness, at least a little bit—the ginger ale, the chicken soup, the extra attention, the daytime television—my kids don't see much romance in ill health. The first thing they want to know about any ailment is, Can you die from it? No? Okay, can I go now?

And they absolutely abhor hospitals. I had to beg them, bribe them and finally almost shove them into the revolving door to visit my sister and her brand-new baby in the maternity ward last summer, their distrust runs so deep. "It smells eewy in here, I can't stand it," Hayes kept saying, though I couldn't detect any odor that alarming. A few months later, when he chopped his finger with a pair of garden shears, he seemed to be more worried about going to the emergency room than about the quarts of blood pouring out of his hand. The saving grace of the ordeal was that he finally caught up with his little brother, who was only three when he split his chin on a trampoline and had stitches and had been lording it over the un-stitched ever since.

As a kid, I saw a great many doctors. My mother, while no sucker for illness, was a connoisseur of cor-rection—whatever was crooked was made straight; what was flat, arched; what was crazy, calmed; what was fat, slimmed. Prominent eye doctors in far-off New York City were charged with re-energizing my lazy eye, while orthopedists were retained for my feet and a trayful of allergy shots were administered by our family doctor on a weekly basis. I saw a diet expert, an orthodontist, a speech therapist, and ultimately, a kiddie shrink. Even plastic surgeons were interviewed.

No matter what their specialties, the drear of their offices and waiting rooms—the toxic green walls, the unnatural lighting, the speckled linoleum—was usually similar. For diversion, they typically had a single copy of *Highlights,* which you'd read the first time you came in. In the hospital where I had my eye operation at the age of seven, I, too, smelled something strange—like a weird kind of food I had never had before, along the lines of canned tomato soup but much more cloying, mixed with something I can only describe as the smell of black plastic. I suppose it was just the aroma of institutional food preparation, but it fascinated rather than repelled me. It made me think romantically of orphanages.

The current custom of tailoring pediatric medical environments to kids had not caught on back then. It has helped quite a bit with Hayes and Vince, who despite their fears can't help but be won over by the efforts of their various doctors. The pediatrician has a cool aquarium and the Disney Channel, the dentist has video games and bubble-gum-flavored nitrous oxide, and the orthopedist who treats Hayes's scoliosis wears Lion King ties and has sports memorabilia on the walls in every room. I was charmed to note they all still have *Highlights* in the waiting room, and it's the same as ever—the Timbertoes, Goofus and Gallant, Hidden Pictures. It could be that issue from 1965 I read so many times.

Thank God—and knock wood, and kenahora, and don't look at me you evil eye, you—Hayes and Vince so far have been marvelously healthy since birth. After going through the loss of their stillborn older brother, it felt like a miracle to deliver Hayes pink and breathing. When the Baby Messiah was born, I was interested to notice he had a pair of webbed toes on his right foot. Though the doctor said it was nothing, not a problem or a bad sign, it reminded me all over again to take nothing for granted, not toes or fingers or hearts or brains or breath.

While so far I've been spared the scary and serious, we've been through all of the normal stuff—and, in at least one case, the not so normal. Because of my neurotic inability to throw away leftovers or waste provisions, the inside of our medicine cabinet is a sort of tour of past illnesses. The untaken antibiotics for the ear infections and bronchitis, a few drops of the special bath formula for chicken pox, cough syrups and antacids, burn sprays and calamine, ointments for warts and rashes. I even have herbal tinctures like Osha and Saint-John's-wort from my brief days almost a decade ago as an all-natural mom. And about a dozen half-empty bottles of, um, lice treatment shampoo.

Shall I go into this? After all, there are subjects one doesn't broach in high-minded literary works, much less at the dinner table. I understand that. A few years ago, I couldn't have pictured myself sipping a cup of coffee and Sambuca at a friend's house, debating the efficacy of various techniques for ridding one's household of lice. But as a member of the ever-growing number of parents who know more about bodily vermin than they ever dreamed possible or necessary, that's exactly what I was doing.

When children in Dublin or Bombay come down with lice, the treatment is simple: they have their heads shaved. But here in the land of plenty, the procedures are a bit more sophisticated. We have products—expensive shampoos for our heads, sprays for our infested furniture, nit-pickers for hire, informational pamphlets and videos, and, of course, a whole psychology of head lice to go with it. In fact, like Elizabeth Kubler-Ross in her study of death and grieving, my friends and I have been able to identify several distinct phases a person typically goes through in coming to terms with this experience. Kubler-Ross has five phases; we came up with ten. Which is typical of head lice. There's always twice as many as you would think.

PHASE 1: DISBELIEF

You get a call from your child's school or day care center or perhaps from the parent of a friend warning you, in apologetic tones, that your little one may have head lice. You must check for nits, their dastardly offspring, almost as invisible as they are invincible. You pay absolutely no attention as they go on to describe the procedure for doing so, since you know this simply is not possible. No one in the history of your family has ever had head lice. No one you *know* has ever had head lice. They must be wrong.

PHASE 2: HUMILIATION

Shortly after the phone call, you observe the child in question scratching his or her head. The first time, you tell yourself it's the creme rinse you're using. Too much chlorine in the pool? However, as the scratching becomes more frequent and vigorous, you can no longer deny the truth. He has head lice. Oh, shit. How did they say you were supposed to check? Didn't they mention some special shampoo? Oh God, the mortification at the drugstore. Not to mention the school and the neighbors and everyone who came to that slumber party.

What about those parents who so kindly kept your kids overnight so you could go out last weekend? Do you really have to call them, too?

PHASE 3: ACCEPTANCE

Once you know how to check for nits—you look for a minuscule whitish bubble stuck to the hair shaft an inch or two from the scalp, usually behind the ears or at the nape of the neck—you learn the extent of the horror. The day of the louse has dawned. You have lice, your spouse has lice, all God's chilluns have lice. If you are lucky, not so many have hatched out that you are treated to the spectacle of scores of gross brown bugs crawling all over your loved one's head.

PHASE 4: CONFIDENCE

Fortunately or unfortunately, it's not just your family. It's your kids' friends, and the friends' parents, and you're all in this together. You'll find out what to do, you'll do it, and it will all soon be just a distant memory. Following the instructions on the lice kit you buy at the grocery store, you wash all the bedding in your house in hot water and bleach. You spray the couches and pillows with the handy can. You have everyone over for a delousing party to scrub each other's hair with the shampoo and comb it out after with the plastic nit comb. See, all better. The kids are playing in the backyard, the grown-ups are inside drinking wine and cracking jokes, the clean sheets are back on the beds, and everything is fine.

PHASE 5: INCREDULITY

A few days later, you're a little itchy. That damn lice shampoo probably dried out your scalp. Then you notice that all those kids sitting in front of your television watching *Animaniacs* are scratching too. The beginnings of a frown appear on your face as you call one of them over, bend his head, and submit him to lice surveillance. Your frown deepens as you go through the strands of hair one by one, finding oodles of tiny bubbles. Welcome back to Nit City. You reach for the phone.

"Anybody itching over at your house?" you ask your friend, trying to remain calm.

"Um, I'm not sure," he replies uncertainly.

"Well, start checking," you say grimly. "They're back."

PHASE 6. RAGE

Okay, now you're pissed. You're not just pissed, you're serious. You're not just serious, you're determined. You're on the horn to the doctor. Isn't there some horribly toxic prescription-only venom you can get to put an end to this plague? Why yes, there is. And it comes complete with two pages of warnings in six-point type about the dire consequences of allowing a single drop of the poison to spill onto skin, eyes, cooking utensils or the foundation of your home, with dire imprecations against applying it more than once every ten days, and disclaimers from the manufacturer about the effects of even the slightest misstep in observing these detailed precautions.

You, who have been carefully purchasing pesticide-free fruits and vegetables for your precious babies since birth, set your jaw, pull on your rubber gloves, and in sheer desperation, pour the vile goop directly onto their sweet little heads. Then you drive straight to the nearest barbershop, biting your lip as the curls fall to the floor. On the way home, you have the interior of the car steam-cleaned. Then you sterilize everything in the linen closet, spray noxious pesticide all over your couch, and surreptitiously carry their favorite baseball caps out to the trash.

It has not been easy, it has not been fun, but you have prevailed.

Phase 7: Blame

No! NO! NO!!!!! This has gone too far. You've done everything. EVERYTHING! And they're back again. No more Mr. Nice Guy. No more namby-pamby-I'm-so-sorry-but. This time, it is not your fault. So whose fault is it? What about these friends of yours? Did they really do their bedding? Did they do the nit thing after the shampoo thing? Perhaps it's the cat. Yes, that must be it. You're all set to take the family pet to the pound when you learn that animals don't carry lice. Well, then it must be the day care center or the school or the summer camp. They aren't really washing those rest mats after all. You, however, are washing your sheets for the fiftieth time in three weeks and SOMEONE MUST PAY.

Phase 8: Craziness

While one friend is making jokes about the kids growing up to play in bands with names like the Scratching Heads and Itchy Scalp, another is deciding whether to relocate to Alaska or Vermont. Is there a listing in the almanac for head lice per capita by state? A divorced couple devises a plan whereby she keeps the kids for ten days while he delouses his house, then he keeps them for ten while she delouses hers. Neither grown-up can share his or her bed with anyone else during the twenty-day quarantine. The purpose of this, like so many agreements forged between the divorced, seems only to torture each other.

Meanwhile, someone is spraying the phone with Lysol.

PHASE 9: MATTER-OF-FACTNESS

By now, you can detect and dispatch a new generation of lice with no more horror than attends the slapping together of a peanut-butter-and-jelly sandwich. You carry a high-tech forged aluminum nit comb complete with 5x magnifying glass in your back pocket at all times, and are not ashamed to whip it out when you observe characteristic scratching behavior even among mere acquaintances or strangers. You can delouse your house and family in under two hours. You have twenty handy boxes of lice shampoo, fifteen cans of bug spray. When considering a sleepover at the home of another group of vermin victims, the only question is this: Have you already washed the bedding? Because if not, I won't bother with the shampoo until tomorrow.

Lice, big deal. It could be worse.

PHASE 10: WORSE

Friend A's cleaning lady finds maggots in his driveway. Friend B withdraws her three-year-old from preschool after receiving a notice regarding an outbreak of giardia. You, on the other hand, get a call from the school nurse informing you that both your kids have a contagious form of pinkeye and are being sent home immediately. Unfortunately, you can't pick them up, as you have locked the keys to the car in the trunk. What is this, the Old Testament? Are there kits at the drugstore for locusts, frogs and boils? At least you have the teen years to look forward to, when you'll be dealing with problems you're familiar with, like unwanted pregnancy, venereal disease, and drug addiction.

Raising children is not for the fainthearted. Right from day one, they've got you suctioning mucus out of tiny baby nostrils with a pale blue rubber squeeze ball. Next, you're up to your elbows in Number One and Number Two. Chicken pox can be a real gross-out, as I recall, as can stomach viruses and poison ivy, and I won't say another word about head lice.

Except this. I wish I knew about them when I was a kid. Because with head lice you're *not allowed* to go to school.

12

Blending

I don't think there's much doubt that two parents are better than one. But while single parenthood is not the ideal, married parenthood is no nonstop party either. Raising a child is the most serious, complex, long-term and emotionally intense project you can undertake with another person, collaboration can be as challenging as going it alone.

For example, the other day on the hike-and-bike trail, my friend Betsy and I were discussing our attempts to control our tongues and tempers in dealing with our children's misbehavior. Both of us admitted to fighting an uphill battle. She told me a story about her husband's intervening in an argument between her and her son that ensued when she turned off an annoying radio station during dinner. Her seven-year-old turned it back on. She turned it off. He turned it on. By the time her husband walked into the room, she was shouting, "Touch that dial and you'll never hear another note of music in your life."

"At that point, Hank came in like some Zen master Dick Van Dyke," she recalled, still fuming at the memory. "He picked Henry up, carried him back to the dinner table and let him sit on his lap. Later, when I tried to explain to him how he was undermining my authority and why the way he handled it just made matters worse, he said, 'When I see you abusing our children, I have to step in.' Can you believe it?"

I could certainly imagine how she felt. Her husband had managed to skate right past the real issue—Henry's rebellious behavior—while making Betsy the problem child and himself the knight in shining armor.

On the other hand, I wondered wistfully, is it so bad to have somebody to step in when you're losing it?

Hayes and Vince turned four and six the year their father died, the year Robb came into our lives. To them, he was Katie and Julie's father, the guy who sat next to me on the bench when we all met at the playground.

The next phase for them began after Tony's death, when he started sleeping over at our house, eating meals with us, either by himself or with Katie and Julie. This transition can feel dangerous to a single mom, especially if she's not sure how long a particular guy is going to be around and she has to wonder how to present him to the kids, what to let them see, and how attached to let them get.

Somehow I never worried about this, never even considered that Robb might be a short-term fling. And Hayes and Vince were little enough when I started sleeping with him that the big issue wasn't who *I* was sleeping with, it was who *they* were sleeping with. Their dad hadn't been around for months; the three of us had been camping out in my bed. At first, they weren't happy about being evicted. Not only were they naturally jealous of Robb's position in my affections and attentions, they were also unused to having someone around with such firm ideas of how children should behave. If Vincie threw a four-year-old hissy fit at the dinner table, Robb would literally pick him up and carry him outside until he agreed to act like a human being. If Hayes tried to whine his way past some limit I had set, Robb would give me a look that shamed me into holding the line. But if I started relying on him too much for disciplinary support, then he felt I was making him into the bad guy.

Over the years, it's become clear that we have different parenting styles; sometimes they blend, sometimes not. At its worst, my style could be described as the Five C's: Coax, Cajole, Curse, Cry, Cave. Robb's is more like *Father Knows Best* meets Mussolini. Results talk: mine are darling boys, but they don't exactly listen to their mom, and will try just about anything to get their way. Katie and Julia, those adorable young ladies, are almost always perfectly behaved, polite, and considerate. They not only love their daddy, they obey him. It's a pretty awe-inspiring act if you've never seen it.

While most of the time I am abjectly grateful for any assistance Robb can give me, there are moments when I am defensive and resentful. I feel so embarrassed about him witnessing my boys' bad behavior and my ineffective reaction to it that it just adds to my stress. Here I am, making one parenting mistake after another and there he is, watching—not only because he doesn't want to undermine my authority, not only because he's not their father, but also because he doesn't know whether I want him to help or whether I'll tell him, as I once did, to "butt out of my world." And then it's not just a discipline problem, but a rift between us.

For example, on the plane ride to our Canadian vacation two years ago, Vincie was loudly ungrateful for the kiddie hot dog meal I had special-ordered for him. Instead of allowing the flight attendant to take it away with the rest of the trays, I asked her to leave it, hoping to persuade him to have a few bites. I had no success in this and ultimately, the untouched tray sat there so long that sheer entropy, and Vincie's squirming, dumped it on the floor. "I'm hungry, Mommy, I'm hungry," Vincie wailed, as the hot dog rolled to the front of the plane. By this time, passengers nearby were giving us looks.

Robb was wincing and I was watching him wince while I tried to pacify Vince, brightly suggesting solutions and distractions, hopefully waylaying a full-scale tantrum. Eventually, wheedling failed and I moved him to another seat, where he continued to make a level of commotion most undesirable on an airplane. "I know you think this is my fault," I hissed at Robb, who was pretty frustrated himself and finally moved across the aisle to stretch out and read. I stared out the window with tears in my eyes, at wit's end.

More recently, we took all four kids to a happy-hour show at a south Austin blues club. Because we knew the owner and the manager, Steve and Gaby, as well as the members of the band, Mrs. Fun, and because it was early evening, we assumed the kids would be welcome. When we arrived, Steve explained this wasn't quite the case. Actually they usually didn't allow children even at early shows, but this one time, it would be all right. I promised they'd behave, and they did, sipping sodas, listening to the music, and shooting pool. At the end of the first set, Gaby sought a kiddie volunteer to take around the band's collection jar. She said she'd pay, in the form of a free Coke. Both Katie and Vincie volunteered. Gaby gave Katie the jar and told Vincie maybe he'd get a chance after the second set.

Katie did a fine job, and got her Coke. Shortly after that, the bar began to fill up. Night was falling; it was clearly time to go. "But I didn't get to do my job!" objected Vince. "And Katie got a Coke! It isn't fair!"

"Come on, Vince," Robb called, herding the kids toward the door. "It's time to leave."

"No! I didn't get my turn!" With this, Vince threw himself under the pool table.

At this point, in Robb's book, the kid was finished. Out of luck, let's go. To me, it seemed that we had told Vince he could do it, he was patiently waiting to do it, and only now that we had betrayed him was he freaking out. My instinct was to try to somehow come through.

"This is ridiculous," said Robb, as I got the tip jar from Gaby. "We'll be waiting outside."

I had Vincie do a fast, unnecessary, midset collection, Gaby gave him a Coke, and we went out to join the others.

"Vincie got an extra soda?!" Hayes shouted in disbelief. "I want another one, too!"

Now Vincie was happily sipping his drink, but Hayes had to be dragged to the car, and the opinion that I had handled the situation incorrectly was written all over Robb's face. Robb's absolute rule of thumb is, Don't reward bad behavior, no matter what. But I can never help seeing the child's point of view.

Robb believes that some of the differences between us arise from basic differences between men and women, ones that can meld in a positive way when a couple raises children together. Daddies teach independence, mothers nurture, he says. I think the first time he expressed this idea, I laughed at his Neanderthal views on gender. These days, I think he's got a point. I'm really good at love and fun, it's all the rest of it I need help with. So why don't I marry the guy, if he'd have me? If we got married, he would be their stepfather and presumably take on the rights and responsibilities thereof.

We'd certainly have no more scenes like that on the airplane or in the Continental Club.

My mom was only fifty-four when my father died, but remarriage never seemed high on her agenda. She got herself a boyfriend, a nice widower from the golf club, who escorts her to all the major dos and wingdings, who takes her out for Chinese and to the early-bird movie, who drives her to the airport when she comes down to Texas to visit me—then kiss kiss, bye-bye, thank you very much, he goes home to his own domicile.

I see my mother as a member of the spare-me-the-dirty-socks school of romance management, to which I myself am something of a convert. How many times do you have to get married to see what sharing living quarters, bank accounts, and laundry hampers can do to a relationship?

My mother and I are decision makers, if not control freaks, with our own homes and cars, our own credit cards and mutual funds. We rule our little islands as uncontested queens. We don't ask anyone's opinion on whether to fix the hot water heater or buy a new one. We don't take input on the destination of our next vacation, or the size of our phone bill. We just do what we want. After all we've seen and been through, is it so surprising we're a little gun-shy about plighting our troth to someone else's health and/or financial problems? Between disallowed income tax shelters, reluctant insurance companies, ancient unpaid parking tickets, and other such memorabilia, can't you really get all the marriage you ever need the first time around?

Except in the case of my sister, whom we want married off as soon as possible.

My sister Nancy, two years younger than I, was widowed last year. She is a truly single single mother.

Not only does she not have a boyfriend, but with two kids in diapers, a full-time job, and a big house in Hackensack, New Jersey, to take care of, she has no time to go out and get one. At this point, going on a date would be about like taking a trip to Europe, in terms of overhead, anticipation, and general extra-ordinariness. Which is not to say she wouldn't happily go.

My sister has a great attitude about her situation, which seems to me to be as tough and unfair as they come. Her first husband died of AIDS. Three years later, her second husband died in an accident, when their son Noah was just sixteen months old and she was seven months pregnant with their new baby. (What was God thinking here? I have to keep asking.) Yet Nancy never seems to feel sorry for herself, she never just lies down on the floor and falls apart. She just keeps on keeping on for those two little boys and for herself. And when a psychic recently told her that the right man would come along in due time, it seemed to echo something she already knew inside.

It's my mother and I who are doing the hand-wringing here. We worry about Nancy. We want her to have somebody. Someone to listen to her, to talk to her, to rub her feet at night after the boys are in bed. Someone to take her to a movie once in a while. Someone for her to celebrate her birthday with, to take out her PMS on, to pick her up from the dentist when she has a root canal. Someone to sit next to her at the eventual school plays and baseball games, to hold her hand outside the inevitable emergency rooms. Someone to love her, and to love those kids with her.

"You've got to put on a little lipstick when you go to the gym, Nancy," I advise her.

"She's an accountant! She does taxes! She visits clients! There's no telling who she could meet," my mother theorizes hopefully. Amazingly, that's what the psychic said too.

However, with the mortality rate for husbands in this family, I'm not sure who would be brave enough to marry any of us.

Unlike my sister, I have been spared the roughest aspect of single parenthood—being truly single. Whatever his reasons and God bless him for them, Robb has been letting me take out my PMS on him for close to three years.

Robb and I didn't get together as much as collide. He later compared our meeting to that between a mobile home and a tornado, or the iceberg and the Titanic. I was the twister and the big ship. In the final throes of what would have been a marriage on the rocks if it weren't also the end of my husband's life, I was half out of my mind. I had felt very alone for a long time.

Robb, too, was alone. Though separated from his wife for six months, his divorce was not final, either on paper or in his heart; he was still consumed with sorrow and anger. He fought to keep his family together and when that failed, fought to make sure he got equal custodial rights. But he was tired of fighting, and already tired of his second bachelorhood. The mood swings and psychodrama of the dating game were not his cup of tea. Like I said, he was the iceberg and the trailer.

If I were writing about him three years ago, before I was quite so used to everything wonderful about him, I would be swooning. So let me swoon a little. It began quite unexpectedly in a restaurant, where we were the first to arrive for a lunch that was to include another writer and the editor of a travel magazine we all contributed to. This was not the first time we'd set eyes on each other—I had run into him over the years, even talked with him about an article I was thinking of writing for the food section he edited at the local paper, but I never really paid much attention. He was married with two kids to a pretty redhead, and I was happily married myself.

Well, he was no longer married, I was no longer

happy and that day at Louis 106, my gaze fell on him and stayed there. He seemed unlike any man I'd been attracted to before. He was big, masculine, and Irish-looking, with blue-green eyes under bushy brows, a street-fighter nose, a bristle-brush mustache above a full lower lip. I liked that mustache. I liked his hair, too, which curled boyishly over the collar of his black leather jacket. Suddenly, I was even intrigued by the two *b*'s at the end of his name.

Halfway through the lunch, which included several bottles of wine, I fed him a shrimp from my bowl with my fingers.

After I became a widow, I had the chance to really get to know the guy with the mustache.

I had certainly been right in thinking that he was unlike any man I'd been attracted to before, including and especially Tony. This was no "sexually ambiguous ice-skating bartender," as I had described my James Dean–esque husband when I first met him. This was a man who watched college football on television, a golfer, a whisky drinker, something of an old-fashioned guy on gender and lifestyle issues. He was a food and wine snob, a born-again carnivore, and as a parent, a strict disciplinarian. A person who would never, for example, pierce his ear.

He was not my type in any way. In fact, in many respects, he drove me crazy and I him as well, and it was impossible to say which of us was the more stubborn, bossy and used to being in charge.

For some reason, all this made both of us very happy.

Robb had done so much for me and my children through our long trials, and as it turned out I was able to do something for his family as well. His relationship with his ex-wife was extremely strained when we first started seeing each other; he could barely bring himself to be civil to her in their phone calls and interactions involving their daughters. For a few months, I took over much of the contact—his ex-wife was a nice Jewish girl from Connecticut and we got along just fine. It was no problem for me to pick up the phone and help work out the summer camp arrangements. But then as Robb started being more happy than mad, he found he could make his own phone calls, and before we knew it we were attending her fortieth birthday party as a couple. He even offered to cook her a lobster dinner, the way he used to do.

We achieved true nineties-hood this past spring, when Cindy had me, my then-visiting mother, and all the kids over for a Passover Seder. The big Catholic fellow who brought us all together sat at the end of the table in silent amazement, watching his thoroughly modern extended family munching matzoh.

According to tradition, Vincie as youngest was charged with reading the ritual questions from the Haggadah. "Why is this night different from all other nights?" he asked.

Robb caught my eye with a look that said, Don't get me started.

Everybody knows little boys need a father. Somebody to toss the ball with. Someone to be a role model. Someone to discipline them. To show them how to be a man, how to be loved by a man, how men love. Someone to look up to. Once their real father is gone, it's a miracle if you can find someone who's right for you and who can do all this too. On television and in the movies, it looks simple. The blended families are smooth as milk shakes. But in real life, everything about stepfamilies, even pseudo-stepfamilies like ours, is very complicated.

Can anybody ever fall in love with your kids the way you want them to? It seems almost unrealistic to hope for it, at our age and stage in life. If the guy doesn't have kids, he probably doesn't want them. If he already has some of his own, at least he's amenable to kid activities and family fun. But it may also mean that his parenting desires are fulfilled. How many more does he need?

There are moments when I feel so hopeful. Like when I see Robb and Hayes walking up the fairway together, or Robb bending over him to reposition his grip. When he carries a sleeping Vincie up from the car. When the boys go out in their nightshirts to kiss him good night. When he comes to sit in the bleachers and watch their soccer games. When he takes them after school to get me a Mother's Day present. When the six of us do something together, and we are so much a family, and the kids play happily together for hours and the lines about who belongs to whom become happily blurred. When I see how much Hayes and Vince take for granted his presence, and his affection, in their lives. Katie and Julie already have a mother. I'm just an added bonus. For the boys, Robb is all there is.

Yet there are times when he walks in the house, goes right by them without saying hello and they don't look up either. When the three of them are just competing for me instead of relating to each other. When he's so fed up with my lax parenting habits that he seems ready to ditch all of us. I have no idea if our living together or getting married would fix this, or make it worse.

The last three years have brought me more happiness than I could have ever dreamed possible. So much that I, who have rushed into every single thing I've ever done in my whole life, including this relationship, am finally taking my time before making changes that could upset the apple cart.

I used to think single mothers were saints; now I see that any parenting arrangement has its challenges. If raising children alone is a juggling act, raising them in a couple is a pas de deux requiring incredible flexibility and grace. The not-so-single parent faces both challenges: keeping the balls in the air while she learns to dance.

3:00 A.M.

FIRST: the smell of baby shampoo, a body sense of being high off the ground. Then: an unfamiliar blanket beneath my cheek, clothes, blue jeans, dried-out contact lenses, a little head on the pillow beside me, Deion Sanders grinning in the darkness—okay, now I get it. I fell asleep in Hayes's bed.

The junior insomniac seems to be down for the count. I linger a minute over his face—those eyelashes, that long plane of cheek, that handsome nose and slightly sultry lower lip; his resemblance to his father grows stronger all the time, and it makes me so happy to see it, as if it were a surprise Tony had left for me to find. A treasure map. A way of never having to say the last goodbye.

I climb down the ladder as quietly as I can and check on Vincie, sprawled on his tummy across a sky blue sheet with hot-air balloons printed on it, his covers kicked off in the warm Texas night. His face is turned sideways, his mouth slightly open, his breathing deep and slow. Asleep, this kid could be on the ceiling of the Sistine Chapel. Even his little white tushie is that of an angel boy. An angel boy who never listens to his mother when she tells him to put on some underpants.

I notice the fourth member of the family has joined the slumber party this evening: Rocco the Giant Cat is sleeping beside Vince, stretched the whole length of his leg. He opens one topaz eye as I pass.

In the kitchen I go to the refrigerator and stand in its cool humming light, tipping the gallon jug of milk to my lips and pouring the cold creamy whiteness right down my throat. I can only drink milk at three in the morning, and only out of the jug—this is the best way to eat things you don't really eat, like fattening dairy products or leftover pepperoni pizza.

Something furry is rubbing against my leg. "Okay, Rocco, but it's not on your diet," I tell him, splashing some milk into his bowl.

Since my mother isn't here to yell at me, I throw my clothes on the floor next to my bed, take out my contacts, set the alarm clock, and burrow under the quilt. The main objective is not to get too awake. Not to start worrying, or planning, or making decisions. Not to start agitating about misunderstood comments or incomplete projects or very important things I have to do right away, none of which I will remember in the morning, though I may remember the clever mnemonic device that was supposed to help me remember them.

It seems strange for a moment that I am alone in this dark house all by myself with these two kids. This is it. Just us. Did they really mean to leave me in charge? This is actually a very big bed to be sleeping in alone.

It sure is quiet.

It sure is dark.

A leap, a heavy landing—tabby attack. Rocco plants himself on my chest, purring loudly, and starts licking my face with his scratchy tongue.

Just when you thought you were all alone in the world, you realize the cat is taking care of *you*.

13

On the Implications
of Birth Order
in Personality Development
or
This Book Unfair to Vince!

Hayes got to go to a real NFL football game of Dallas against the Minnesota Vikings, but Vince didn't because his mother said she wasn't spending that kind of money to send somebody to something he doesn't even like. That was totally unfair. Even though his mother rented a canoe and took him out on Town Lake and then let him choose out any restaurant he wanted for lunch and when he picked "the secret restaurant that's famous for noodles" and she actually figured out what he had in mind—a Thai place located in an alley—so? Big deal. It's still unfair. Hayes got souvenirs! What did Vince get?

Hayes has about nine soccer trophies and Vincie only has four because his mother said he couldn't sign up for soccer unless he actually got out there and played and didn't just wander around the sidelines with Gabe's baby brother Nay-nay.

How come Hayes got new sneakers and Vincie didn't?

Vincie's birthday is in July when school is out and he's almost always up at his nana's house in New Jersey and he never gets to have a regular party with his friends from school, the kind where every single person brings you a present. This year his mom let him have a half-birthday party in January but then she went around telling people that small presents under five dollars would be fine. She said you can't just declare any old day your birthday and order people to come over and give you presents. Well, why did she even have to have Vince in July? Why couldn't she have him in April like Hayes? Hayes got to take cupcakes to school on his birthday!

It's not fair that Vincie's mother used to hate football but now she likes it and Vincie has no one to hate football with, and it's not fair that Uncle Frankie gave Hayes a whole bunch of trading cards and he just gave Vincie like two. Okay, ten. Whatever, it wasn't fair.

Everyone keeps trying to throw away Vincie's

favorite shirt, which was once Day-Glo green with Day-Glo orange sleeves, but now is kind of faded and spotted and one sleeve and the collar are coming off. It has a really awesome picture of a surfer and the words SURFIN DUDE on it, and it used to go with some shorts that had one orange leg and one navy blue leg but they disappeared. Leave Vincie's stuff alone! Don't throw away his clothes!

There were only four cookies left and Vincie's brother ate three of them and their mother didn't do one single thing. That is it. Vincie is leaving.

And where, may I ask, is Vincie's boat? For years—years!—he has been telling them he wants a boat, and no one ever gets him one. Not a stupid rubber raft like they gave him two years ago! He wants a boat, not a toy. Made of real wood. With paddles.

Vincie had a guinea pig named Sparky that his kindergarten teacher Mrs. Coffee gave him but his mother left his cage out on the front porch without a cover and he ran away and got lost but he still might come back. His mom had a cat that ran away when she was a little girl and it came back. So you never know.

Vince got Rollerblades for his birthday and then the next year Hayes got Rollerblades for his birthday. Guess why this is unfair. Because Hayes's are brand-new! Vince's are old! And just wait: I bet she tries to give Vince this old pair of Hayes's when he grows out of them.

When his mother sent Vincie to art classes at the museum, Hayes got to come too, even though Vincie didn't get to go that football game.

Vincie told his mother not to sing that song she made up about poo-poo and woo-woo anymore, and then she goes and puts it in her stupid book.

Hayes got a watch!

Vincie knows the facts of life because Calvin told him. Yeah-huh, did too. A man and woman take off their clothes and get in bed together and he puts his peenuss in her pachina and some stuff comes out and turns into a baby. And you know what it's called? It's called S-E-X!

Vincie's mom is a liar. She said he could choose out anything he wanted with his five dollars of Geoffrey money from Toys "R" Us but hardly nothing in that store costs five dollars! She always lies!

Look, Vincie's chapter is only four pages long. The whole book is about Hayes! Duh!

14

Holiday Hell

Shortly before Christmas a couple of years ago, I found Hayes sitting at the kitchen table staring into his cereal bowl, pushing a single Frosted Mini-wheat around in the remaining milk. Such relative motionlessness was a dead giveaway. Something was on his mind.

"What's the matter, scrunchmuffin?" I asked.

"Mom," he asked, peering anxiously at me through his overgrown bangs, "have I been good?"

"Well, pretty good. Not perfect, but certainly not terrible." Now this is odd, I thought, until it hit me. "Why, baby, are you thinking about your Christmas presents?" I reached over and tried to push his hair out of his eyes.

"Kind of. I don't want to get a Diet Coke in my stocking," he muttered, shrugging.

"A what?"

"A Diet Coke. Davey Walsh told me that if you're

not good, Santa Claus leaves a Diet Coke in your stocking. And Davey knows."

I bet he does, that little rascal. I hated to laugh at such a serious moment of self-examination but it was too much. A Diet Coke?

Under our questioning, Robb's eleven-year-old nephew Davey maintained that he had in fact passed on the more traditional story, that the stocking of a naughty child might be found on Christmas morning to contain nothing but a lump of coal. The miscommunication still got the message across. In fact, in our modern world, the specter of low-calorie soda might be even more effective in eliciting good behavior than would that of virtually obsolete fossil fuels.

Or as Hayes later put it, "Lump of coal, Diet Coke, whatever."

Due to such threats or not, my kids were not much trouble this past December. Most of the time they were planted in front of the television, shouting the names of toys seen in commercials to be added to their growing number of Christmas requests. Finally, I had them sit down and write letters to Santa Claus, planning to make off with the lists and read them to doting relatives over the phone.

Robb's kids were over that night, and all four of

them were intently bent over their papers at the table, Katie's shiny dark head, Julie and Hayes's sandy ones, Vincie's in a backwards baseball cap with bangs sticking out the front. As the littlest, he pooped out first from the effort of writing big long phrases like "Star Wars Luke Skywalker Light Saber," so everybody took turns helping him out. "I have been very good this year," each letter assured Santa.

"Or should we put 'mostly good'?" Hayes agonized.

The letters were folded and placed in envelopes addressed to the North Pole, and I even gave out real thirty-two-cent stamps to put on them. I figure as long as Daniel Dominguez's mother hasn't confessed that she's also Santa Claus, we might as well go all the way. After we'd carried the letters to the mailbox, ten-year-old Katie paused on the front steps and gave me a look.

"You know, Marion, I really *want* to believe in Santa Claus," she sighed, "I want to, but it's getting harder every year."

Ah, well, my little Katie, give it about thirty more and see what happens. I, too, want to believe in Santa Claus. A big guy in a red suit to take over this deal for me—that would be great. But at this point, my holiday challenge is to believe that a tired lady in a white nightgown with coffee stains down the front can get the job done. My grumpy old self as elf.

Even before I was a single mom, I was not what you would call a holiday person. I hated the holidays for all the normal reasons—the enforced hominess and happiness, the mandatory doing and going, and most of all, the relentless theme-iness of it all, the holiday colors, the holiday plants, the holiday Muzak, the tinkly-winkly sappiness belabored to death everywhere you look. The usual grinchy objections. But being alone with two kids has added new dimensions to the dread, which typically sets in shortly before Thanksgiving and continues through New Year's.

The worst thing about being a single parent during the holidays is not the effort and stress of trying to pull off the various required elements by yourself. That's minor, compared to the emotional part, which is about like lining up to get onto Noah's Ark without a mate: you can't help but notice something's missing. No matter what your religious background, the Norman Rockwell–style painting of your happy family has a hole in it. And despite the general festivity and cuteness of everyone and everything around you, you cannot achieve true jollyhood, no matter how hard you try.

Even if you really think you want to be independent and you can handle it and it's better this way, Christmas is the time of the year when, if you're not careful, you end up proposing to the homeless guy sitting on the curb outside the video store when you come out with your rented copy of *It's a Wonderful Life*.

For a girl from a nice Jewish family, I have a long history with the celebration of the birth of Christ. This is because my parents were not very Jewish Jews, at least in terms of observances and rituals. To make sure we learned something about our heritage, they dutifully joined a temple and sent us off to Hebrew and Sunday school when we were small—and then were stuck with various enthusiasms we came home with. Mom, let's have our own seder! Can we, Mom, please? Can we build a sukkah in the backyard? Do we have a menorah? It turned out she did have one— up on a dusty shelf in the garage, her mother's actually, featuring a brass Lion of Judah supporting the nine candleholders. And so Hanukkah was added on to our winter holiday omnibus sometime during my elementary school years. While the major gift-giving was saved for December 25, we got smaller presents—barrettes or Crazy Eights card decks or hand-held staplers—on the nights of Hanukkah.

Christmas was the more long-standing tradition in our home, which we celebrated not as Christians, but as Americans. We decorated our house not with lights and plastic manger scenes, but with the seemingly hundreds of greeting cards my parents received every year and stuck up in the moldings around the walls of the den. My mother spent weeks checking and updating her Christmas card list and addressing envelopes. The holiday season was a time of reckoning in my parent's social life—everyone who sent a card received one in return, and those who went more than two or three years without being heard from were crossed off.

"Forget the Frankenweilers," my mother would announce, drawing a line through their name with a flourish of finality. "Ever since they moved, it's like we dropped off the face of the earth."

"Get this!" chortled my father, brandishing a card from the stack. "The Percy Gryces wish us Hanukkah happiness! Very broad-minded of them! Did we send to them?"

We children, too, were hard at work on our lists, for we were lucky little girls. Every Christmas morning, we would awaken to twin altars of presents, high as the ceiling and wide as an ocean to our dazzled young eyes. If we did not get the exact same gifts, we would at least get a strictly equivalent number and size of boxes, and always identical would be the Big One, the Grand Finale, found all the way back at the source of this river of toys: two bicycles or two record players, two portable black-and-white televisions or pink princess phones.

We would work our way back through the piles, box by box, opening the presents in choreographed sequence, while our parents watched, filled with the fun of giving things to children who want things that can actually be had, and whose joy at receiving them is such a great reward. I can see my parents sitting on the couch in their bathrobes, grinning, sharing glances of anticipation, gloating over the success of their surprises, reaching out to accept our exuberant hugs and kisses.

In the afternoon, we would pile into the car to go to my aunt Joan's house in a hilly, horsey area of north Jersey. At Aunt Joan's, they went all the way—a silver bowl of eggnog, a giant evergreen in the living room, my uncle Louis coming down the staircase dressed as Santa. Were they even Jewish? I wondered as a child. Yes, it turned out, just a little more "reformed" than we were.

I got all the Christmas I could ever want when I married Tony, not only a bona fide Catholic but the son of a woman who was a raving Christmas fanatic. The customs of ornaments, crèches, decorations, cooking, shopping and wrapping were observed at nearly fetishistic levels in his childhood household, and as an adult he did his mama proud.

Even before we had kids, we always had a tree, decorated with Mexican tin ornaments and old sparkly glass ones. He adorned the house with *papel picado* garlands; he cut boughs of greenery and arranged them around votive candles. He set out pots of cinnamon potpourri, for God's sake. Martha Stewart had nothing on this man. After our kids were born, things were even more full-tilt, the orgy of preparations culminating with our staying up half the night on Christmas Eve wrapping presents and drinking champagne, selections from Tony's holiday CD collection—Barbra Streisand, Disco Christmas, medieval Gregorian chants—on five-disk shuffle in the background. The next morning we'd sit on the couch with our coffee cups, just like my parents, watching our darling little boys open the presents, and in the afternoon, we'd have friends over for lasagna and mulled wine.

Out of nostalgia for my almost-heritage, I introduced Hanukkah when the kids were little, though it was Tony who tooled over to the gift shop of a nearby synagogue to choose the perfect menorah, then located hand-dipped candles at Clarksville Pottery. I taught Hayes and Vincie the Hebrew prayers, and like my parents, gave little presents—temporary tattoos, oil pastel sets, X-Men action figures. Good old Hanukkah, with its evening ritual and its simplicity. I liked it so much, I even went so far as to make latkes.

After Tony died, it was clear to all concerned that I would need lots of help maintaining the style of Christmas to which Hayes and Vince were accustomed. Ever since the first year, my in-laws have driven all the way from Pennsylvania in early December to make sure things get off on the right foot. They send me away for the weekend while they buy and set up a tree. They haul out the ornaments, set up the choo-choo, and decorate the house inside and out, complete with strings of blinking lights on the roof and a wreath on the door. They purchase vast numbers of gifts for the boys, wrap them, tag them and hide them under my bed, which by the time I come home is flanked by Russian Santa Claus dolls. They drive the kids around to look at Christmas lights and to visit Santa at the mall and even to buy their grinchy old mother some presents.

Thanks to my in-laws' thoroughgoing efforts—they sweetly, and probably truthfully, insist that they love doing it—I'm able to maintain a skeptical semi-sourpuss attitude as everyone around me gets with the program in the weeks that follow. I certainly don't have to decorate, and all the shopping that's still required can be accomplished in three hellbent hours at Penney's and Toys "R" Us.

On the cooking-and-baking end of things, I can count on Robb, who loves the holidays almost as much as Tony did, but whose energies are expressed in the kitchen. He bakes cookies with the kids, experiments with gloggs and nogs, and on Christmas Eve puts on a twelve-course, vegetarian traditional Slavic meal, complete with unbelievably good mushroom-barley soup and bales of hay spread on the floor. The next day he serves up roast beef, Yorkshire pudding, and burgundy for Christmas dinner, and in between we've got the Shahins' tamale breakfast Christmas morning. You would think there would be no time amidst all the face-stuffing for me to break down.

And I didn't in years prior, because each year my mother came in shortly after the in-laws left. She would be there on Christmas Eve to wrap presents and drink champagne, and would wake up with me and the boys on Christmas morning to share the fun. But this year she had to stay in New Jersey because it was my sister's first Christmas alone, and in her absence, I finally hit holiday bottom. Wrapping those presents by myself, unable to find the Barbara Streisand CD, drinking flat Diet Dr. Pepper, I felt as single as a single parent can feel. When I ran out of

Scotch tape with three more presents to go, that was it. I walked out the front door into the chilly dark and stood staring at the stars. Hope the wise men are coming with the tape, I thought. My red-and-green-flashing house seemed to be sending a Morse code of holiday distress into the silent night.

But before I knew it, New Year's Day arrived. Which meant the holidays were officially over. Once again, I had survived. And it was a brand-new year. Beset by just a slight hangover, I went gingerly into the kitchen and started to make coffee. Within seconds, the sounds of a scuffle emerged from the boys' room. The door banged open and Vincie raced through the kitchen with Hayes hot on his heels.

"Give me my light saber!"

"Mom, he's gonna kill me."

"That one's mine. You broke yours!"

"Ma! Help!"

Certain no serious mayhem would ensue, I chose my escape route. Balancing a cup of coffee, a pad and a pencil, I waited until their chase took them to the opposite part of the house and tiptoed out the front door. There I clambered over the milk crates, empty pet cages, jumper cables, sports equipment and bags of old clothes destined for Goodwill, and lowered myself into a wicker rocker so battered Goodwill has actually refused to accept it. "New Year's Resolutions," I wrote at the top of the page. "1. Clean porch."

And then I looked around and sighed. That was on the list last time. And the time before, probably. I realized I felt the same way about New Year's resolutions as Katie does about Santa Claus. I want to believe—but it's getting harder every year. Having seen myself fail abysmally or partially, immediately or eventually, in every resolve, I'm finding it a little harder to pull myself together to make them.

Wasn't this the year I was never going to raise my voice again? (The only way I can see this happening is if I get some sort of operation.) And let's see, I was going to wake up every morning and be the nicest, sweetest mommy in the whole world. I was never going to swear at them or "go mental" as Hayes gently puts it. I was going to clean their rooms and organize their bookshelves. Meanwhile I was going to lose weight, exercise every day and eschew any and all remaining bad habits.

What I realized on that messy front porch of mine is that I can't bear to go through this rigmarole anymore. Instead of resolving, and setting myself up for failure, I decided I'd be better off to aspire. Aspirations are something you live with, like two volumes of *War and Peace* on a bookshelf or a pair of size six jeans in the back of the closet. Even if you haven't quite gotten into them, you don't throw them away. You keep them around, you keep trying, slowly, slowly, you make progress toward them and you never know— someday you may arrive.

To be a parent is a form of ongoing aspiration. The love we feel for our children is so pure and so good, we can only aspire to be equal to it in our lives and deeds. It isn't easy. But it isn't optional, either. We are parents, and we have to live with that. And live up to it.

Otherwise, you know what we'll get.

Diet Coke.

6:15 A.M.

Hayes Winik   February 17, 1997
English

Good Cop, Bad Cop

In the morning, it is a nut house at my house. The first thing I do in the morning is get dressed while my mom is screaming at my lazy brother in bed. The second thing I do is eat breakfast while my mom is still yelling at my lazy brother. The third thing I do is watch T.V. while my brother is finally getting dressed and eating breakfast. The fourth thing we do is drive to school in our green jeep. My mom would go crazy if I were as lazy as that brother of mine!

Even with my eyes closed, I sense the soft light in the room, filtered through rice paper blinds as through veils of sleep. I think of this as the gray area: the time of the morning when I'm not quite asleep anymore and I know the alarm will go off soon but I'm definitely not opening my eyes or going anywhere until it does.

Suddenly, the veils are swept aside by something clear and definite: the sound of someone peeing in my bathroom. Hopefully into the toilet, but you can never be sure around here. When this person completes his morning whiz, he will undoubtedly climb on his mother's bed and crawl in beside her, for in the gray area, getting in Mommy's bed is allowed.

He does, and the veils descend again, a few minutes of deep sleep at the eleventh hour, and then beep-beep-beep-beep-beep-beep! I reach over to silence the clock and find my glasses.

"Good morning, Mr. Hayes," I say, opening my eyes. Hayes's big brown eyes, liquid and shining, are very close to mine.

"Good morning, Mama," he says, beginning to crawl over me. "Time to get up."

"Go wake up Voo-dog," I tell him.

"Yeah, right," he says. The project of getting Hayes to go to sleep at night is nothing compared to the project of getting his little brother up in the morning.

"What do you want for breakfast? How about birdie eggs?" Birdie eggs features a nest of torn-up toast topped with crumbled bacon and two soft-boiled eggs, quite a favorite around here. My mother used to make this for me growing up, but we didn't call it birdie eggs. That I got from Katie and Julie, whose mother and aunt named it that when they were little girls because you tear up the bread the same way you do to feed the birds.

Breakfast is the only meal I cook with true enthusiasm. I like the limited choices, the limited number of pots and dishes to clean up, the limited amount of time and decorum required. Breakfast is easy: if you manage anything much more complex than a bowl of cereal, you're a hero and a gourmet.

"Yeah, birdie eggs," Hayes agrees.

"Go get dressed, babe."

On the way to the kitchen, I stop in the boys' bedroom to inaugurate the Vincie wake-up project. I flick on the overhead light and lie down beside him for a second. He is hot, heavy and pink with sleep. On some level of consciousness he realizes what is going on, and tries to scurry deeper into slumber to avoid it.

I start tickling him below the ear. He smiles a little. I do it more.

"Cut it out, Ma!" He spits it out like Linda Blair in her darkest moments of demonic possession.

Here we go again. I pat him softly on his angel tush and sigh.

Taking a break from the exorcism, I go in the kitchen to make coffee, layer bacon with paper towels in the microwave, and start boiling water.

"Hayes, are you dressed? Could you go outside and get the paper?"

No answer. "Hayes?"

Still nothing. "Hayes? Where are you?"

He's on the couch watching cartoons stark naked.

"No television until you get dressed, young man. Excuse me—am I talking to the wall?" Here I go again, just like my mother. I walk over and turn off the television.

"Maaaaaaa," he whines. True fingernails-on-the-blackboard style.

I feel myself start to lose it. I see the morning veering off like a train wreck in progress. Faster than a speeding baseball, more powerful than a temper tantrum, able to turn a kindly caretaker into a snapping grump in a matter of seconds—it's the Waging Whinoceros, with his petulant, pathetic, tremulous, broken-record whimper, and his little brother, the Demon Spawn from Hell.

It's not the words themselves; it's the sound effects. Whining makes you want to remove the batteries from your child. Sometimes I think I would respond more calmly to the news that nuclear war had broken out than I do when these kids whine at me.

"Maaaa, I don't waaaaant to get dressed."

"Go get dressed right now," I tell him through gritted teeth. I'm walking the edge of a spillway here.

I can just feel words I don't want to say trying to come out of my mouth.

Morning is far and away the most intense part of my parenting day. For a while, around the time Tony died, it was so bad I actually went to a counselor to help me figure it out. You would have thought I needed help with our grief and bereavement. Instead, I needed help with getting their shoes on. The counselor suggested we put a big chart on the wall with times of day and steps listed in order. From 6:30 GET UP to 7:25 BRUSH TEETH to 7:35 LEAVE HOUSE.

That worked for a while. Then after that, I had some deal worked out where you got to watch a cartoon if you were ready in time. That gave way to a cash incentive program: I'll pay you to put your clothes on and eat this waffle! Everything works for a while, but nothing works forever.

Let us now skip ahead twenty minutes or so, sparing you many capital letters and exclamation points, and assume that Vincie is up. (If Robb were here, he would have put an ice cube in his underpants during this period.) He comes out of his bedroom and joins Hayes at the breakfast table. They both start to chow down on their birdie eggs.

You might think my troubles are over—but no. Perhaps Hayes will now notice that Vincie is wearing some clothing item of his. Or Vincie may start making some annoying noise over and over. Or they could just skip the causation part and go straight to hitting and screaming at each other.

"Finish your breakfast," I urge them as I begin gathering lunch items. I pull Bart Simpson out of the drain rack and deal out the fruit roll-ups, the chips, the apples, the salami sandwiches, and the tinfoil-wrapped kosher dills. Thirty-five cents for milk, taped to a quickly scribbled note. "Brush your teeth! Comb your hair! Put your shoes on! For Pete's sake, boys, move!"

I'm drinking cup after cup of coffee, which is probably only making it worse. I have to get these two kooks out of here and get started on my horrible day, which I deserve because I'm such a horrible mother. The only thing that could make matters worse is if we don't get to school before the late bell—to me a sign of complete failure as a parent. The other half of this equation is a bedtime story. No matter how disastrous everything is, if I get them to school on time and put them to bed with a story, I somehow feel that all is not lost.

"Can I tell you something?" I announce when there's a break in the action. "You boys are destroying my nerves."

"What are nerves?"

I'm thinking of how to explain this when the conversation switches to another track.

"Vincie said the B-word!"

"What's the B-word? Oh, forget it, I don't even want to know."

"It's boo-tocks," Vince informs me. "Hayes is a pain in my boo-tocks!"

I suppress the giggles I feel coming on. "Put on your shoes," I say firmly, "brush your teeth and let's get out of here!"

Without even getting up, they both shout: "Mom, I can't find my shoes!"

I'm ready for this. "They're in my room. Right next to the door."

"Could you get them for me?"

"I guess you didn't get to the part in school where they freed the slaves in this country, Hayes. Now come on, let's go! Let's go! Pick up your shoes, get your backpacks and leave the house! To the Jeep! To the Jeep! You can put your shoes on on the way!"

It's 7:33 and we're getting out of here. Yippee. Then I look down at myself and see that in all the excitement, I have neglected to get dressed and now am driving to school in a white nightgown, truly glamorous eyeglasses and insane-looking hair. If we get in an accident, I'll probably be institutionalized.

But who cares? We are on our way! I see Tomi Dominguez and Daniel in the rearview mirror. Tomi Dominguez has on a nice brown suit and jewelry and does not look like the Madwoman of Chaillot. I scrunch down a little as she pulls up next to us at the light.

As soon as I stop in the drive at the school, the boys have the door open.

"Wait! Can't I get a kiss goodbye?"

But now they aren't thinking about me. They're ready for their friends and their classes and the world. I won't even cross their minds until they find the notes that say "I love you" in their lunch boxes. (That moron Mom strikes again!) They make little kissing faces from the sidewalk as they turn away.

"Bye, Mom," they call in unison.

Bye, boys. I bet this is what it's going to be like when they leave for good, too. I bet you never get your kiss. I bet they never even say goodbye.

Uh-oh. Here comes that PTA fund-raising lady with a big smile on her face. Gotta run.

ACKNOWLEDGMENTS

Thanks to my late husband Tony, his parents Grace and Rod, my mother Jane and late father Hy, and all the family members on both sides who have given so much to me and my children.

For their much leaned-on camaraderie, thanks to the Walshes, the Shahins, the Ducotes, the Dominguezes, the Burnetts, and the many other dear friends, teachers, and staff at Bryker Woods Elementary. Thanks to Dolly Barclay and the ladies of the Book Club. God bless you, Erika Allbright.

Continued gratitude to my wise ambassadors in the world of publishing, Patricia Van der Leun and Robin Desser, and a special thanks to Marty Asher. For their assistance with the writing of this book, thanks to Margaret Low Smith, Deborah Kirk, Dawn Raffel, Dana Joseph Williams, Barrie Gillies, Melissa Chesser Aspell and Margaret Moser.

Thanks, finally, to my sons Hayes and Vince, who wrote all the good lines.

ABOUT THE AUTHOR

Marion Winik has been a regular commentator on National Public Radio's *All Things Considered* since 1991. She has published in *Redbook, Harper's Bazaar, Parenting, American Way* and many other magazines. The author of *Telling* and *First Comes Love,* she lives in Austin, Texas, with her sons.